DIABETIC RECIPES

Eat your favorites while managing your diabetes

pil

Publications International, Ltd.

Pictured on the front cover (*clockwise from top left*): Oatmeal with Maple-Glazed Apples and Cranberries (*page 22*), Creamy Farmhouse Chicken and Garden Soup (*page 54*) and Barley and Vegetable Risotto (*page 266*).

Pictured on the back cover (*left to right, top to bottom*): Cran-Orange Acorn Squash (*page 256*), Roasted Tomato-Basil Soup (*page 41*), Apple-Cherry Glazed Pork Chops (*page 126*), Breakfast Quinoa (*page 14*), Mu Shu Turkey (*page 192*) and French Carrot Medley (*page 302*).

ISBN: 978-1-68022-691-1

Library of Congress Control Number: 2016946223

Manufactured in China.

8 7 6 5 4 3 2 1

Nutritional Analysis: Every effort has been made to check the accuracy of the nutritional information that appears with each recipe. However, because numerous variables account for a wide range of values for certain foods, nutritive analyses in this book should be considered approximate. Different results may be obtained by using different nutrient databases and different brand-name products.

Microwave Cooking: Microwave ovens vary in wattage. Use the cooking times as guidelines and check for doneness before adding more time.

Preparation/Cooking Times: Preparation times are based on the approximate amount of time required to assemble the recipe before cooking, baking, chilling or serving. These times include preparation steps such as measuring, chopping and mixing. The fact that some preparations and cooking can be done simultaneously is taken into account. Preparation of optional ingredients and serving suggestions is not included.

Note: This book is for informational purposes and is not intended to provide medical advice. Neither Publications International, Ltd., nor the authors, editors or publisher takes responsibility for any possible consequences from any treatment, procedure, exercise, dietary modification, action, or applications of medication or preparation by any person reading or following the information in this cookbook. The publication of this book does not constitute the practice of medicine, and this cookbook does not replace your physician, pharmacist or health-care specialist. Before undertaking any course of treatment or nutritional plan, the authors, editors and publisher advise the reader to check with a physician or other health-care provider.

Not all recipes in this cookbook are appropriate for all people with diabetes. Health-care providers, registered dietitians and certified diabetes educators can help design specific meal plans tailored to individual needs.

TABLE OF CONTENTS

p. 18

p. 124

p. 278

HEALTHY EATING

In order to manage your diabetes, it's important that you understand what causes your disease and why the foods you eat play an important role in its control and treatment.

There are two types of diabetes mellitus: type 1 insulin-dependent diabetes mellitus, (also known as juvenile diabetes), and type 2 diabetes mellitus, (formerly known as non-insulin dependent diabetes mellitus or adult-onset diabetes mellitus). While the causes of these diseases are different, the role that food plays in your management of each disease is the same.

DECIPHERING THE TERMS

After we consume a meal, the foods we eat are broken down during digestion into glucose. This is important because the energy we need to live comes from the glucose in our bodies. Glucose provides the power for every body function, whether it's walking, lifting weights or sleeping. The term "blood glucose" is often used interchangeably with "blood sugar," as glucose is a simple form of sugar.

Excess glucose that isn't used for energy right away is stored in the muscle, liver and fat tissues for later use. Insulin is a hormone that is responsible for taking the glucose that has been released into the bloodstream after digestion and storing it into the muscle, liver and fat cells.

For those with type 1 diabetes, the pancreas is not able to produce insulin; consequently, blood glucose produced by digestion continues to circulate in the bloodstream. In type 2 diabetes, the pancreas produces insulin but the muscle, liver and fat cells that should accept the glucose from insulin do not function properly and will not take in what is circulating in the blood. The glucose then remains within the bloodstream. This is known as "insulin resistance."

LIVING WITH DIABETES

Increased levels of blood glucose can cause serious medical complications, including excessive thirst, hunger, blurred vision, weight loss and dehydration. In fact, these symptoms typically lead someone to consult a physician and ultimately to their medical diagnosis.

Medicine often plays a role in diabetes maintenance. People with type 1 diabetes cannot produce insulin themselves, so they require an intravenous pump or injections to provide the insulin needed to transfer glucose from the blood to the cells. Some people with type 2 diabetes also require supplemental insulin and many take drugs to assist in the upload of glucose from the blood to the tissues.

Although medical treatment varies from person to person, diet is a major component in the treatment plan for anyone with diabetes. The best way to educate yourself about the disease and its treatment is to consult with your physician, a registered dietitian and/or a Certified Diabetes Educator to create an individualized diabetic meal plan that suits your physical requirements and your lifestyle. You will then be able to make responsible choices and still take pleasure in eating the dishes you have always treasured.

FOOD BASICS

Whether you are dealing with type 1 or type 2 diabetes, it's important to be aware of exactly what and how much you're eating. It's also crucial to know the effects that various foods have on your blood glucose levels.

The fuel that our bodies use as energy is Calories. Calories come from four main sources—carbohydrates, protein, fat and alcohol—and each of these sources affects your blood glucose levels differently. In addition, most foods are not comprised of only fat or only carbohydrates; thus, it's important to look at the Nutrition Facts Panel on a package or the nutrition information listed on a menu or recipe to be sure of exactly what you're eating. We will be looking only at the nutrients that pertain to the recipes in this book—carbohydrates, protein and fat.

Carbohydrates are the primary nutrient found in breads, pasta and cereals, and they make up approximately half of the calories we consume. Carbohydrates are also the greatest contributor to our blood glucose levels. If someone were to consume a piece of white bread, he or she would experience a spike in blood glucose levels soon after. This is because our digestive process breaks down carbohydrates easily and rapidly.

Often, people with diabetes try to control their disease by restricting the amount of carbohydrates they consume. However, eliminating food groups is never a good idea—control of the disease comes from knowing what types of foods to eat and which nutrients to look out for.

Your protein consumption should also be considered. Protein—found in lean meats, fish, soy, fat-free or low-fat dairy products, beans and nuts—is digested comparatively slowly. As a result, eating foods with a significant amount of protein makes us feel full sooner and satisfied longer after we eat. Additionally, when protein is eaten with carbohydrates, the protein delays the blood glucose response.

There is a lot of speculation on where fat fits within the diet. For many years fat was considered to be bad, something to be restricted, but this is not necessarily true. While fat does contribute more calories than equivalent amounts of carbohydrates or protein, certain types of fat have been proven to have health benefits.

The types of fats to limit are saturated fats and trans fats, commonly found in butter, cheeses, meats and other animal products. These types of fats have been found to increase levels of LDL cholesterol (the "bad" cholesterol) in the body and therefore are strongly connected to your risk of heart disease. On the other hand, mono-unsaturated fats and poly-unsaturated fats—present in sources such as avocados, vegetable oils and fish—have been found to improve heart health by decreasing LDL cholesterol levels in the body, as well as reducing inflammation.

Despite the popularity of a "fat-free" diet, there is clearly no need to eliminate fat, but to watch the type and amount consumed, as it's a large source of calories. Replace foods in your diet that may be high in saturated or trans fats with those that are higher in unsaturated fats. For example, sauté your vegetables in olive oil instead of butter, and replace some meat with fish that is higher in unsaturated fats, such as salmon.

THE FACTS OF FIBER

Dietary fiber is a key component to the success of any diet. Fiber has been proven effective in disease prevention, weight loss and blood glucose control. It's naturally present in plants and therefore is a major nutritional component of fruits, vegetables, beans, nuts, seeds and whole grains. Dietary fiber is what leaves us feeling satisfied after we eat a large apple or vegetable salad.

SUBSTITUTING GOOD FATS FOR BAD FATS

1. Cook with olive oil. If you need flavorless oil, try canola or grapeseed oil. If the recipe requires the rich taste of butter, you can usually replace half of it with oil without compromising the flavor.

2. Prepare it yourself. Store-bought salad dressings and sauces can be loaded with sugar, sodium and preservatives. Make a simple vinaigrette or marinade with olive oil, or just pass a good quality vinegar and olive oil at the table.

3. Avoid processed meat. It is not only loaded with sodium, it may also be high in fat.

4. Choose low-fat dairy. Drink low-fat milk and cook with low-fat dairy products. Watch out for cheese, as it can contribute to a lot of saturated, or "bad," fat to your diet. Try using small amounts of full-flavored cheeses like Parmesan or feta.

5. Cook at home. It is no secret that foods prepared at restaurants are not good for us; they're loaded with hidden ingredients and the portion sizes are huge! Eating out makes us take in higher amounts of fat, carbohydrates, sodium and calories.

Dietary fiber slows down the process of digestion, which helps in a couple of ways. First, our brains get time to decide we're full and signal us to stop eating. Additionally, by delaying the digestive process, dietary fiber slows down the breakdown of food to glucose, moderating the blood glucose rise that occurs after any meal.

There are two forms of dietary fiber that you may see on food labels—insoluble and soluble fiber. While both are classified as fiber, their benefits differ.

Most of the fiber we consume is insoluble fiber. This type of fiber increases the weight and size of your stool, which allows regular bowel movements to occur, preventing constipation and aiding in digestive health. (If you want to increase fiber in your diet, just be cautious not to add too much too quickly or increase the amount of fiber in your diet without increasing your water intake, as well. A drastic increase of fiber in the diet can cause abdominal discomfort, gas and constipation.)

Soluble fiber also has significant health benefits. This type of fiber—found mostly in beans, oats and the peels of apples—absorbs water. This absorption provides a feeling of fullness as you eat, which helps you avoid overeating. This type of fiber also slows down the digestive processes, again helping to delay the blood glucose response after a meal.

Soluble fiber plays an important role in heart health, too. When bound to water,

HIGH FIBER FRUITS AND VEGETABLES
(per 1-cup, unless otherwise indicated)

Avocado, cubed	10g
Green Peas	9g
Raspberries	8g
Acorn Squash	6g
Pear, large with skin	6g
Apple, large with skin	5g
Corn	5g
Potato, medium, baked with skin	5g
Asparagus	4g
Carrot	4g
Orange	4g
Spinach, cooked	4g
Strawberries	4g
Banana, medium	3g
Broccoli	2g
Grapefruit, ½ of whole fruit	2g

soluble fiber forms a gel-like substance in the digestive tract. In this form, it absorbs cholesterol, which is then carried out of the body. This reduces your blood cholesterol levels, helping to reduce your risk of heart disease.

Both types of dietary fiber play an important role in weight loss. Insoluble fiber increases the bulk in our stomach, while soluble fiber slows down the digestive processes. As a result, we feel fuller from a smaller amount of food for an extended period of time.

While many processed food products do have some added fiber, the best sources are natural, unrefined foods such as fruits, vegetables, whole grains and beans—common ingredients in many of the recipes in this book.

PUTTING IT ALL TOGETHER

In a nutshell, carbohydrates break down easily during digestion. When you eat a food high in carbohydrates, your blood glucose will rise quickly. Fat and protein also break down into glucose, but they'll go through many more steps at the cellular level before this occurs, and thus don't cause the spike in blood glucose levels that carbohydrates do. In fact, when carbohydrates are eaten along with some protein or fat, the blood glucose response is delayed.

Most people are much more likely to eat a food or a meal that consists of a combination of carbohydrates, protein and fat than of a single nutrient alone. Therefore, paying attention to each of these elements within a meal will assist in blood glucose control.

For example, when you eat a turkey sandwich, the protein from the turkey will delay the response that the carbohydrates in the bread would normally have on blood glucose levels if eaten alone. (To delay the response further, eat whole wheat bread, full of dietary fiber, which will leave you feeling full and satisfied until your next meal.)

PORTION DISTORTION

Regardless of what you're eating, one of the most important things that you should

FIVE EASY WAYS TO INCREASE THE FIBER IN YOUR DIET

1. Start out strong. Choose a high fiber hot cereal with fruit for breakfast.
2. Switch to whole grains. Try brown rice, whole grain pastas and breads.
3. Eat the whole fruit. The fiber is in the peel and the pulp.
4. Drop the peeler. Instead, scrub apples and potatoes and cook with the peel on.
5. Get big on beans. Eat beans or lentils three times a week. They're loaded with fiber.

pay attention to is portion size. Whether your guide is the serving size listed on the Nutrition Facts Panel on any packaged food or the nutrition information listed at the bottom of the recipes in this book, portion size is always pertinent.

For instance, you may pour yourself a bowl of cereal with milk for breakfast. Ideally, you also may see that the serving size listed on the Nutrition Facts Panel is 1 cup—but chances are, the amount of cereal in your bowl is not 1 cup. Additionally, the amount of milk that you added to that cereal will need to be considered if you want to know, for example, how many total calories were in that bowl of cereal. Learning to recognize all of the ingredients in a dish and the recommended serving sizes are fundamental tools to the success of any diet.

Portion control is particularly crucial for people with diabetes in order to maintain their blood glucose levels within a healthy range. Many people with diabetes will focus on their carbohydrate amounts and space their consumption throughout the day. This type of meal plan will help to prevent large spikes in blood glucose levels, as the goal for managing diabetes is to keep your blood glucose levels at a steady, consistent level at all times.

A HEALTHY WAY OF LIFE

This book is a guide and a resource for helping you create some of your favorite dishes in your **CROCK-POT®** slow cooker and fit them into a healthy meal plan. The nutrition information is provided with each recipe in this book so that you'll be aware of how each dish will affect your blood glucose levels and fit within your diabetic diet. The nutrition information listed is based on a single serving and does not include garnishes or optional ingredients; when a range is given for an ingredient, the nutritional analysis reflects the lesser amount. Please consult a registered dietitian or health care provider who can offer nutrition advice, tips and meal plans that are all specific to you, your health condition and your lifestyle.

TIPS FOR ADDING VEGGIES TO YOUR DIET

1. Make it easy on yourself. Choose prewashed bags of vegetables or bring home goodies from the salad bar at the local supermarket.

2. Go vegetarian once a week. Plan a whole meal around a vegetable-based main dish. Try a soup, stew or pasta creation.

3. Cook with more veggies. Add veggies to your favorite dishes, like zucchini or carrots, in meat loaf or breads.

4. Try something new and different. Add color and flavor to your menus with less mainstream vegetables. Try mustard greens, beets or different varieties of more common veggies such as Italian-style green beans.

5. Grow your own or shop locally. Grow vegetables in your garden or visit a farmers' market or produce stand. You will be exposed to all different types of vegetables that you'll want to start cooking with. Plus, eating fresh fruits and vegetables is a great way to get your vitamins.

Italian Stew, p. 187

SLOW COOKING 101

CROCK-POT® SLOW COOKER SIZES

Smaller slow cookers—such as 1- to 3½-quart models—are the perfect size for cooking for singles, a couple or empty-nesters (and also for serving dips).

While medium-size slow cookers (those holding somewhere between 3 quarts and 5 quarts) will easily cook enough food at a time to feed a small family, they're also convenient for holiday side dishes or appetizers.

Large slow cookers are great for large family dinners, holiday entertaining and potluck suppers. A 6- to 7-quart model is ideal if you like to make meals in advance, or have dinner tonight and store leftovers for another day.

TYPES OF CROCK-POT® SLOW COOKERS

Current **CROCK-POT®** slow cookers come equipped with many different features and benefits, including auto cook programs and timed programming. Visit **www.crock-pot.com** to find the **CROCK-POT®**

slow cooker that best suits your needs. How you plan to use a **CROCK-POT®** slow cooker may affect the model you choose to purchase. For everyday cooking, choose a size large enough to serve your family. If you plan to use the **CROCK-POT®** slow cooker primarily for entertaining, choose one of the larger sizes. Basic **CROCK-POT®** slow cookers can hold as little as 16 ounces or as much as 7 quarts. The smallest sizes are great for keeping dips hot on a buffet, while the larger sizes can more readily fit large quantities of food and larger roasts.

COOKING, STIRRING AND FOOD SAFETY

CROCK-POT® slow cookers are safe to leave unattended. The outer heating base may get hot as it cooks, but it should not pose a fire hazard. The heating element in the heating base functions at a low wattage and is safe for your countertops.

Your **CROCK-POT®** slow cooker should be filled about one-half to three-fourths full for most recipes unless otherwise instructed. Lean meats such as chicken or pork tenderloin will cook faster than meats with more connective tissue and fat such as beef chuck or pork shoulder. Bone-in meats will take longer than boneless cuts. Typical **CROCK-POT**® slow cooker dishes take approximately 7 to 8 hours to reach the simmer point on LOW and about 3 to 4 hours on HIGH. Once the vegetables and meat start to simmer and braise, their flavors will fully blend and meat will become fall-off-the-bone tender.

According to the USDA, all bacteria are killed at a temperature of 165°F. It's important to follow the recommended cooking times and not to open the lid often, especially early in the cooking process when heat is building up inside the unit. If you need to open the lid to check on your food or are adding additional ingredients, remember to allow additional cooking time if necessary to ensure food is cooked through and tender.

Large **CROCK-POT**® slow cookers, the 6- to 7-quart sizes, may benefit from a quick stir halfway during cook time to help distribute heat and promote even cooking. It's usually unnecessary to stir at all, as even ½ cup liquid will help to distribute heat, and the stoneware is the perfect medium for holding food at an even temperature throughout the cooking process.

OVEN-SAFE

All **CROCK-POT**® slow cooker removable stoneware inserts may (without their lids) be used safely in ovens at up to 400°F. Also, all **CROCK-POT**® slow cookers are microwavable without their lids. If you own another brand slow cooker, please refer to your owner's manual for specific stoneware cooking medium tolerances.

FROZEN FOOD

Frozen food or partially frozen food can be successfully cooked in a **CROCK-POT**® slow cooker; however, it will require longer cooking than the same recipe made with fresh food. It's almost always preferable to thaw frozen food prior to placing it in the **CROCK-POT**® slow cooker. Using an instant-read thermometer is recommended to ensure meat is fully cooked through.

PASTA AND RICE

If you're converting a recipe that calls for uncooked pasta, cook the pasta on the stovetop just until slightly tender before adding to the **CROCK-POT**® slow cooker. If you are converting a recipe that calls for cooked rice, stir in raw rice with other ingredients; add ¼ cup extra liquid per ¼ cup of raw rice.

BEANS

Beans must be softened completely before combining with sugar and/or acidic foods. Sugar and acid have a hardening effect on beans and will prevent softening. Fully cooked canned beans may be used as a substitute.

VEGETABLES

Root vegetables often cook more slowly than meat. Cut vegetables accordingly to cook at the same rate as meat—large or small, or lean versus marbled—and place near the sides or bottom of the stoneware to facilitate cooking.

HERBS

Fresh herbs add flavor and color when added at the end of the cooking cycle; if added at the beginning, many fresh herbs' flavor will dissipate over long cook times. Ground and/or dried herbs and spices work well in slow cooking and may be added at the beginning, and for dishes with shorter cook times, hearty fresh herbs such as rosemary and thyme hold up well. The flavor power of all herbs and spices can vary greatly depending on their particular strength and shelf life. Use chili powders and garlic powder sparingly, as these can sometimes intensify over the long cook times. Always taste the dish at end of the cook cycle and correct seasonings including salt and pepper.

LIQUIDS

It's not necessary to use more than ½ to 1 cup liquid in most instances since juices in meats and vegetables are retained more in slow cooking than in conventional cooking. Excess liquid can be cooked down and concentrated after slow cooking on the stovetop or by removing meat and vegetables from the stoneware, stirring in one of the following thickeners and setting the **CROCK-POT**® slow cooker to HIGH. Cover; cook on HIGH for approximately 15 minutes until juices are thickened.

Flour: All-purpose flour is often used to thicken soups or stews. Place flour in a small bowl or cup and stir in enough cold water to make a thin, lump-free mixture. With the **CROCK-POT**® slow cooker on HIGH, quickly whisk the flour mixture into the liquid in the **CROCK-POT**® slow cooker. Cover; cook on HIGH until the mixture thickens.

Cornstarch: Cornstarch gives sauces a clear, shiny appearance; it's used most often for sweet dessert sauces and stir-fry sauces. Place cornstarch in a small bowl or cup and stir in cold water until the cornstarch dissolves. Quickly whisk this mixture into the liquid in the **CROCK-POT**® slow cooker; the sauce will thicken as soon as the liquid simmers. Cornstarch breaks down with too much heat, so never add it at the beginning of the slow cooking process, and turn off the heat as soon as the sauce thickens.

MILK

Milk, cream and sour cream break down during extended cooking. When possible, add during the last 15 to 30 minutes of cooking, just until heated through. Condensed soups may be substituted for milk and can cook for an extended time.

FISH

Fish is delicate and should be added during the last 15 to 30 minutes of cooking time. Cook until just cooked through and serve immediately.

BREAKFAST DISHES

Breakfast Quinoa

1½ cups uncooked quinoa

3 cups water

3 tablespoons packed brown sugar

2 tablespoons maple syrup

1½ teaspoons ground cinnamon

¾ cup golden raisins

Fresh raspberries and banana slices

1. Place quinoa in fine-mesh strainer; rinse well under cold running water. Remove to **CROCK-POT**® slow cooker.

2. Stir water, brown sugar, maple syrup and cinnamon into **CROCK-POT**® slow cooker. Cover; cook on LOW 5 hours or on HIGH 2½ hours or until quinoa is tender and water is absorbed.

3. Add raisins during last 10 to 15 minutes of cooking time. Top quinoa with raspberries and bananas.

Makes 6 servings

Nutrition Information

Serving Size: ⅔ cup

Calories 233
Total Fat.........................3g
Saturated Fat 1g
Protein 6g
Carbohydrate 47g
Cholesterol 0mg
Fiber 4g
Sodium......................9mg

Dietary Exchanges:
2 Starch, 1 Fruit, ½ Fat

Orange Cranberry Nut Bread

Tip

This recipe works best in round **CROCK-POT**® slow cookers.

- **2 cups all-purpose flour**
- **½ cup chopped pecans**
- **1 teaspoon baking powder**
- **½ teaspoon baking soda**
- **¼ teaspoon salt**
- **1 cup dried cranberries**
- **2 teaspoons dried orange peel**
- **⅔ cup boiling water**
- **¾ cup sugar**
- **2 tablespoons shortening**
- **1 egg, lightly beaten**
- **1 teaspoon vanilla**

1. Coat inside of 3-quart **CROCK-POT**® slow cooker with nonstick cooking spray. Combine flour, pecans, baking powder, baking soda and salt in medium bowl.

2. Combine cranberries and orange peel in separate medium bowl; stir in boiling water. Add sugar, shortening, egg and vanilla; stir just until blended. Add flour mixture; stir just until blended.

3. Pour batter into **CROCK-POT**® slow cooker. Cover; cook on HIGH 1¼ to 1½ hours or until edges begin to brown and toothpick inserted into center comes out clean.

4. Remove stoneware insert from **CROCK-POT**® slow cooker. Cool on wire rack 10 minutes. Remove bread from insert; cool completely on rack.

Makes 10 servings

Note

To make foil handles: Tear off three 18×2-inch strips of heavy foil or use regular foil folded to double thickness. Crisscross foil strips in spoke design and place in **CROCK-POT®** slow cooker to allow for easy removal of bread pudding.

Luscious Pecan Bread Pudding

   3 **cups day-old French bread cubes**
   3 **tablespoons chopped pecans, toasted***
2¼ **cups low-fat (1%) milk**
   2 **eggs, beaten**
 ½ **cup sugar**
   1 **teaspoon vanilla**
 ¾ **teaspoon ground cinnamon, divided**
 ¾ **cup reduced-calorie cranberry juice cocktail**
1½ **cups frozen pitted tart cherries**
   2 **tablespoons sugar substitute**

*To toast pecans, spread in single layer in heavy skillet. Cook over medium heat 1 to 2 minutes or until nuts are lightly browned, stirring frequently.

1. Prepare foil handles. See Note. Toss bread cubes and pecans in soufflé dish that fits inside of **CROCK-POT®** slow cooker.

2. Combine milk, eggs, sugar, vanilla and ½ teaspoon cinnamon in large bowl; pour over bread mixture in soufflé dish. Cover tightly with foil. Place soufflé dish in **CROCK-POT®** slow cooker. Pour hot water into **CROCK-POT®** slow cooker to about 1½ inches from top of soufflé dish. Cover; cook on LOW 2 to 3 hours.

3. Meanwhile, combine cranberry juice and remaining ¼ teaspoon cinnamon in small saucepan; stir in cherries. Bring to a boil over medium heat; cook 5 minutes. Remove from heat. Stir in sugar substitute.

4. Lift soufflé dish from **CROCK-POT®** slow cooker using foil handles. Serve bread pudding with cherry sauce.

Makes 6 servings

Sausage and Red Pepper Strata

Nonstick cooking spray

12 ounces reduced-fat bulk pork breakfast sausage

1 teaspoon dried oregano

½ teaspoon red pepper flakes (optional)

8 slices day-old French bread, cut into ½-inch cubes

1 medium red bell pepper, finely chopped

¼ cup chopped fresh Italian parsley, plus additional for garnish

2 cups cholesterol-free egg substitute

2 cups evaporated fat-free milk

2 teaspoons Dijon mustard

½ teaspoon black pepper

1 cup (4 ounces) shredded reduced-fat sharp Cheddar cheese

1. Spray large skillet with cooking spray; heat over medium-high heat. Add sausage, oregano and red pepper flakes, if desired; cook 6 to 8 minutes or until browned, stirring to break up meat. Drain fat.

2. Coat inside of **CROCK-POT**® slow cooker with cooking spray. Add bread. Sprinkle sausage mixture evenly over bread; top with bell pepper and ¼ cup parsley.

3. Whisk egg substitute, evaporated milk, mustard and black pepper in medium bowl until well blended. Pour evenly over sausage mixture in **CROCK-POT**® slow cooker. Cover; cook on LOW 3 to 3½ hours or on HIGH 2 to 2½ hours or until eggs are firm but still moist.

4. Turn off heat. Sprinkle cheese over top. Cover; let stand 5 minutes or until cheese is melted. Garnish with additional parsley.

Makes 8 servings

Nutrition Information

Serving Size:
¾ cup oatmeal,
⅓ cup apple mixture and
1 tablespoon cranberries

Calories 230
Total Fat 4g
Saturated Fat 1g
Protein 6g
Carbohydrate 47g
Cholesterol 3mg
Fiber 6g
Sodium 158mg

Dietary Exchanges:
2 Starch, 1 Fruit, ½ Fat

Oatmeal with Maple-Glazed Apples and Cranberries

  3 cups water

  2 cups quick-cooking or old-fashioned oats

  ¼ teaspoon salt

  1 teaspoon unsalted butter

  2 medium red or Golden Delicious apples, unpeeled and cut into ½-inch pieces

  ¼ teaspoon ground cinnamon

  2 tablespoons sugar-free maple syrup

  4 tablespoons dried cranberries

1. Combine water, oats and salt in **CROCK-POT**® slow cooker. Cover; cook on LOW 8 hours.

2. Melt butter in large nonstick skillet over medium heat. Add apples and cinnamon; cook and stir 4 to 5 minutes or until tender. Stir in syrup; heat through.

3. Serve oatmeal with apple mixture and dried cranberries.

Makes 4 servings

Roasted Pepper and Sourdough Egg Dish

3 cups sourdough bread cubes
1 jar (12 ounces) roasted red pepper strips, drained
1 cup (4 ounces) shredded reduced-fat Monterey Jack cheese
1 cup (4 ounces) shredded reduced-fat sharp Cheddar cheese
1 cup fat-free cottage cheese
1½ cups cholesterol-free egg substitute
1 cup fat-free (skim) milk
¼ cup chopped fresh cilantro
¼ teaspoon black pepper

1. Coat inside of **CROCK-POT®** slow cooker with nonstick cooking spray. Add bread. Arrange roasted peppers evenly over bread cubes; sprinkle with Monterey Jack and Cheddar cheeses.

2. Place cottage cheese in food processor or blender; process until smooth. Add egg substitute and milk; process just until blended. Stir in cilantro and black pepper.

3. Pour egg mixture into **CROCK-POT®** slow cooker. Cover; cook on LOW 3 to 3½ hours or on HIGH 2 to 2½ hours or until eggs are firm but still moist.

Makes 8 servings

Nutrition Information

Serving Size: ⅙ of loaf

Calories 300
Total Fat..................... 12g
Saturated Fat..............2g
Protein 6g
Carbohydrate 46g
Cholesterol 55mg
Fiber 2g
Sodium................. 350mg

Dietary Exchanges:
1 Starch, ½ Fruit, ½ Fat

Note

Banana nut bread has always been a favorite way to use up those overripe bananas. Not only is it delicious, but it also freezes well for future use.

Banana Nut Bread

⅓ **cup unsalted butter or margarine**
3 **medium ripe bananas, well mashed**
⅔ **cup sugar**
2 **eggs, well beaten**
2 **tablespoons dark corn syrup**
1¾ **cups all-purpose flour**
2 **teaspoons baking powder**
½ **teaspoon salt**
¼ **teaspoon baking soda**
⅓ **cup chopped walnuts**

1. Grease and flour inside of **CROCK-POT®** slow cooker. Beat butter in large bowl with electric mixer until fluffy. Gradually beat in bananas, sugar, eggs and corn syrup until smooth.

2. Sift together flour, baking powder, salt and baking soda in small bowl. Slowly beat flour mixture into creamed mixture. Add walnuts and mix thoroughly. Pour into **CROCK-POT®** slow cooker. Cover; cook on HIGH 2 to 3 hours.

3. Turn off heat. Let cool, then turn bread out onto serving platter.

Makes 1 loaf

Nutrition Information

Serving Size: ½ cup

Calories 189
Total Fat 3g
Saturated Fat 1g
Protein 8g
Carbohydrate 33g
Cholesterol 71mg
Fiber 3g
Sodium 206mg

Dietary Exchanges:
1½ Starch, ½ Fruit,
½ Meat

Blueberry-Orange French Toast Casserole

½ cup sugar substitute

½ cup fat-free (skim) milk

2 eggs

4 egg whites

1 tablespoon grated orange peel

½ teaspoon vanilla

6 slices whole wheat bread, cut into 1-inch cubes

1 cup fresh blueberries

Sugar-free maple syrup (optional)

1. Coat inside of **CROCK-POT**® slow cooker with nonstick cooking spray. Stir sugar substitute and milk in large bowl until sugar substitute is dissolved. Whisk in eggs, egg whites, orange peel and vanilla. Add bread and blueberries; stir to coat.

2. Remove mixture to **CROCK-POT**® slow cooker. Cover; cook on LOW 3 to 4 hours or on HIGH 1½ to 2 hours or until toothpick inserted into center comes out mostly clean.

3. Turn off heat. Let stand 10 minutes. Serve with syrup, if desired.

Makes 6 servings

Cherry-Orange Oatmeal

4 cups water

2 cups old-fashioned oats

4 tablespoons sugar substitute

2 tablespoons unsweetened cocoa powder

2 cups fresh pitted cherries or frozen dark sweet cherries

2 cans (11 ounces *each*) mandarin orange segments in light syrup, rinsed and drained

1. Combine water, oats, sugar substitute and cocoa in **CROCK-POT®** slow cooker; stir to blend. Cover; cook on LOW 8 hours.

2. Divide mixture evenly among eight serving bowls. Top with cherries and oranges.

Makes 8 servings

Morning Mocha

Nutrition Information

Serving Size: ¾ cup

Calories 20
Total Fat.........................1g
Saturated Fat 1g
Protein 1g
Carbohydrate 3g
Cholesterol 3mg
Fiber 1g
Sodium....................16mg

Dietary Exchanges:
Free

Note

Mocha may be kept warm in **CROCK-POT**® slow cooker on LOW setting for up to 3 hours.

¼ **cup sugar substitute**
2 **tablespoons unsweetened cocoa**
6 **cups brewed coffee**
1 **cup low-fat (1%) milk**
8 **tablespoons frozen low-fat whipped topping (optional)**
   Ground cinnamon (optional)

1. Combine sugar substitute and cocoa in **CROCK-POT**® slow cooker. Stir in coffee and milk. Cover; cook on LOW 3 hours or on HIGH 1½ hours or until heated through.

2. Stir well before serving. Garnish with whipped topping and cinnamon.

Makes 8 servings

Spicy Apple Butter

5 pounds tart cooking apples (McIntosh, Granny Smith, Rome Beauty or York Imperial), peeled, cored and quartered (about 10 large apples)

1 cup sugar

½ cup apple juice

2 teaspoons ground cinnamon

½ teaspoon ground cloves

½ teaspoon ground allspice

Bread slices

1. Combine apples, sugar, apple juice, cinnamon, cloves and allspice in **CROCK-POT**® slow cooker. Cover; cook on LOW 8 to 10 hours or until apples are very tender.

2. Mash apples with potato masher. Cook, uncovered, on LOW 2 hours or until thickened, stirring occasionally to prevent sticking. Serve on bread.

Makes about 6 cups

Nutrition Information

Serving Size:
2 tablespoons

Calories 20
Total Fat........................0g
Saturated Fat 0g
Protein 0g
Carbohydrate 5g
Cholesterol 0mg
Fiber 1g
Sodium......................0mg

Dietary Exchanges:
Free

Serving Suggestion

Homemade apple butter is a great alternative to store-bought jam or jelly.

Nutrition Information

Serving Size: 1 wedge

Calories 230
Total Fat 6g
Saturated Fat 1g
Protein 5g
Carbohydrate 38g
Cholesterol 15mg
Fiber 1g
Sodium 250mg

Dietary Exchanges:
2 Starch, 1 Fat

Blueberry-Banana Pancakes

  2 **cups all-purpose flour**
 ⅓ **cup sugar**
  1 **tablespoon baking powder**
 ½ **teaspoon baking soda**
 ½ **teaspoon salt**
 ½ **teaspoon ground cinnamon**
1¾ **cups milk**
  2 **eggs, lightly beaten**
 ¼ **cup (½ stick) unsalted butter, melted**
  1 **teaspoon vanilla**
  1 **cup fresh blueberries**
  2 **small bananas, sliced**
    Sugar-free maple syrup (optional)

1. Combine flour, sugar, baking powder, baking soda, salt and cinnamon in large bowl. Combine milk, eggs, butter and vanilla in separate medium bowl. Pour milk mixture into flour mixture; stir until moistened. Gently fold in blueberries until mixed.

2. Coat inside of **CROCK-POT**® slow cooker with nonstick cooking spray. Pour batter into **CROCK-POT**® slow cooker. Cover; cook on HIGH 2 hours or until puffed and toothpick inserted into center comes out clean. Cut evenly into eight wedges; top with sliced bananas and syrup, if desired.

Makes 8 servings

Raisin-Oat Quick Bread

1½ cups all-purpose flour, plus additional for dusting

⅔ cup old-fashioned oats

⅓ cup fat-free (skim) milk

4 teaspoons baking powder

1 teaspoon ground cinnamon

½ teaspoon salt

½ cup packed raisins

1 cup sugar

2 eggs, lightly beaten

½ cup (1 stick) unsalted butter, melted, plus additional for serving

1 teaspoon vanilla

1. Spray inside of ovenproof glass or ceramic loaf pan that fits inside of **CROCK-POT**® slow cooker with nonstick cooking spray; dust with flour.

2. Combine oats and milk in small bowl; let stand 10 minutes.

3. Meanwhile, combine 1½ cups flour, baking powder, cinnamon and salt in large bowl; stir in raisins. Whisk sugar, eggs, ½ cup melted butter and vanilla in separate medium bowl; stir in oat mixture. Pour sugar mixture into flour mixture; stir just until moistened. Pour into prepared pan. Place in **CROCK-POT**® slow cooker. Cover; cook on HIGH 2½ to 3 hours or until toothpick inserted into center comes out clean.

4. Remove pan from **CROCK-POT**® slow cooker; let cool in pan 10 minutes. Remove bread from pan; let cool on wire rack 3 minutes before slicing. Serve with additional butter, if desired.

Makes 12 servings

Nutrition Information

Serving Size: 1 cup

Calories 60
Total Fat 0g
Saturated Fat 0g
Protein 1g
Carbohydrate 15g
Cholesterol 0mg
Fiber 1g
Sodium......................6mg

Dietary Exchanges:
1 Fruit

Spiced Apple Tea

3 bags cinnamon herbal tea

3 cups boiling water

2 cups unsweetened apple juice

6 whole cloves

1 whole cinnamon stick

1. Place tea bags in **CROCK-POT**® slow cooker. Pour boiling water over tea bags; cover and let steep 10 minutes. Remove and discard tea bags.

2. Add apple juice, cloves and cinnamon stick to **CROCK-POT**® slow cooker. Cover; cook on LOW 2 to 3 hours. Remove and discard cloves and cinnamon stick. Serve warm in mugs.

Makes 4 servings

3-Fruit Oatmeal

- **4¼ cups water**
- **1 cup steel-cut oats**
- **¼ cup golden raisins**
- **¼ cup dried cranberries**
- **¼ cup dried cherries**
- **2 tablespoons honey**
- **1 teaspoon vanilla**
- **¼ teaspoon salt**
- **1 cup sliced fresh strawberries (optional)**

Combine water, oats, raisins, cranberries, cherries, honey, vanilla and salt in **CROCK-POT®** slow cooker; stir to blend. Cover; cook on LOW 7 to 7½ hours. Top each serving evenly with strawberries, if desired.

Makes 4 servings

Nutrition Information

Serving Size: ½ cup

Calories 260
Total Fat 3g
Saturated Fat 1g
Protein 6g
Carbohydrate 53g
Cholesterol 0mg
Fiber 5g
Sodium 150mg

Dietary Exchanges:
2½ Starch, ½ Fat

SOUPS

Roasted Tomato-Basil Soup

- **2 cans (28 ounces *each*) whole tomatoes, drained and 3 cups juice reserved**
- **2½ tablespoons packed dark brown sugar**
- **1 medium onion, finely chopped**
- **3 cups fat-free reduced-sodium vegetable broth**
- **3 tablespoons tomato paste**
- **¼ teaspoon ground allspice**
- **1 can (5 ounces) evaporated milk**
- **¼ cup chopped fresh basil**
- **Salt and black pepper (optional)**
- **Sprigs fresh basil (optional)**

1. Preheat oven to 450°F. Line baking sheet with foil; spray with nonstick cooking spray. Arrange tomatoes on foil in single layer. Top with brown sugar and onion. Bake 25 minutes or until tomatoes look dry and light brown. Let tomatoes cool slightly; finely chop.

2. Combine tomato mixture, 3 cups reserved juice, broth, tomato paste and allspice in **CROCK-POT®** slow cooker; stir to blend. Cover; cook on LOW 8 hours or on HIGH 4 hours.

3. Add evaporated milk and ¼ cup chopped basil; season with salt and pepper, if desired. Cover; cook on HIGH 30 minutes or until heated through. Garnish with basil sprigs.

Makes 8 servings

Nutrition Information

Serving Size: about 1 cup

Calories 100
Total Fat 2g
Saturated Fat 1g
Protein 4g
Carbohydrate 17g
Cholesterol 5mg
Fiber 2g
Sodium 620mg

Dietary Exchanges:
2 Vegetable

Nutrition Information

Serving Size: 1¼ cups

Calories 250
Total Fat...................... 12g
Saturated Fat............... 2g
Protein 11g
Carbohydrate 30g
Cholesterol 5mg
Fiber 12g
Sodium................. 750mg

Dietary Exchanges:
1½ Starch, ½ Vegetable,
½ Fruit, ½ Meat, 1½ Fat

Pumpkin Soup with Crumbled Bacon and Toasted Pumpkin Seeds

- **2 teaspoons olive oil**
- **½ cup raw pumpkin seeds***
- **2 slices thick-cut bacon**
- **1 medium onion, chopped**
- **1 teaspoon kosher salt**
- **½ teaspoon chipotle chili powder**
- **½ teaspoon black pepper**
- **2 cans (29 ounces *each*) 100% pumpkin purée**
- **4 cups fat-free reduced-sodium chicken broth**
- **¾ cup apple cider**
- **½ cup fat-free half-and-half**
- **Sour cream (optional)**

*Raw pumpkin seeds or pepitas may be found in the produce or ethnic food section of your local supermarket.

1. Coat inside of **CROCK-POT**® slow cooker with nonstick cooking spray. Heat oil in small skillet over medium-high heat. Add pumpkin seeds; stir until seeds begin to pop, about 1 minute. Spoon into small bowl; set aside.

2. Add bacon to skillet; cook and stir until crisp. Remove bacon to paper towel-lined plate using slotted spoon. Reserve drippings in skillet. Crumble bacon when cool enough to handle; set aside. Reduce heat to medium. Add onion to skillet; cook and stir 3 minutes or until translucent. Stir in salt, chili powder and pepper. Remove to **CROCK-POT**® slow cooker.

3. Whisk pumpkin purée, broth and cider into **CROCK-POT**® slow cooker until smooth. Cover; cook on HIGH 4 hours.

4. Turn off heat. Whisk in half-and-half; strain soup evenly into bowls. Garnish with pumpkin seeds, bacon and sour cream, if desired.

Makes 6 servings

Mediterranean Tomato, Oregano and Orzo Soup

2 tablespoons extra virgin olive oil

1 large yellow onion, cut into wedges

3½ cups fresh tomatoes, peeled and crushed*

2 cups butternut squash, peeled and cut into ½-inch cubes

1 cup carrots, cut into matchstick pieces

½ cup zucchini, sliced

1½ teaspoons minced bay leaves

1 tablespoon chopped fresh oregano

1 can (about 15 ounces) chickpeas, rinsed and drained

2 cups fat-free chicken broth

1 clove garlic, minced

1 teaspoon ground cumin

¾ teaspoon ground allspice

½ teaspoon salt

¼ teaspoon black pepper

1½ cups uncooked orzo pasta

To peel tomatoes, place one at a time in simmering water about 10 seconds. (Add 30 seconds if tomatoes are not fully ripened.) Immediately plunge into a bowl of cold water for another 10 seconds. Peel skin with a knife.

1. Heat oil in large skillet over medium heat. Add onion; cook and stir 10 minutes or until translucent.

2. Add tomatoes, squash, carrots, zucchini, bay leaves and oregano to skillet; cook and stir 10 to 15 minutes. Remove to **CROCK-POT**® slow cooker.

3. Add remaining ingredients except pasta. Cover; cook on LOW 7 to 8 hours or on HIGH 4 to 5 hours.

4. Add pasta. Cover; cook on HIGH 30 to 45 minutes or until pasta is heated through.

Makes 8 servings

Serving Size: 2½ cups

Calories 240
Total Fat 7g
Saturated Fat 2g
Protein 18g
Carbohydrate 29g
Cholesterol 25mg
Fiber 7g
Sodium 670mg

Dietary Exchanges:
1 Starch, 2½ Vegetable,
1½ Meat, ½ Fat

Northwest Beef and Vegetable Soup

> 2 **tablespoons olive oil**
> 1 **pound cubed lean beef stew meat**
> 1 **medium onion, chopped**
> 1 **clove garlic, minced**
> 8 **cups water**
> 3½ **cups canned crushed tomatoes, undrained**
> 1 **can (about 15 ounces) no-salt-added white beans, rinsed and drained**
> 1 **pound butternut squash, peeled and diced**
> 1 **medium turnip, peeled and diced**
> 1 **large potato, diced**
> 2 **medium stalks celery, sliced**
> 2 **tablespoons minced fresh basil**
> 1½ **teaspoons salt**
> 1 **teaspoon black pepper**

1. Heat oil in large skillet over medium heat. Brown beef on all sides. Add onion and garlic; cook and stir 2 minutes. Remove to **CROCK-POT®** slow cooker.

2. Add water, tomatoes, beans, squash, turnip, potato, celery, basil, salt and pepper; stir to blend. Cover; cook on HIGH 2 hours. Turn **CROCK-POT®** slow cooker to LOW. Cook on LOW 4 to 6 hours, stirring occasionally.

Makes 8 servings

Italian Sausage Soup

Sausage Meatballs

- **1 pound bulk mild Italian sausage, casings removed**
- **½ cup plain dry bread crumbs**
- **¼ cup grated Parmesan cheese, plus additional for garnish**
- **¼ cup fat-free (skim) milk**
- **1 egg**
- **½ teaspoon dried basil**
- **½ teaspoon black pepper**
- **¼ teaspoon garlic salt**

Soup

- **4 cups hot fat-free reduced-sodium chicken broth**
- **1 tablespoon tomato paste**
- **2 cloves garlic, minced**
- **¼ teaspoon red pepper flakes**
- **½ cup uncooked mini pasta shells***
- **1 bag (10 ounces) baby spinach**

Or you may use other tiny pasta, such as ditalini (mini tubes) or farfallini (mini bow ties).

1. Combine sausage, bread crumbs, ¼ cup cheese, milk, egg, basil, black pepper and garlic salt in medium bowl. Shape into 16 meatballs.

2. Combine broth, tomato paste, garlic and red pepper flakes in **CROCK-POT**® slow cooker. Add meatballs. Cover; cook on LOW 5 to 6 hours.

3. Add pasta 30 minutes before serving. When pasta is tender, stir in spinach. Sprinkle with additional Parmesan cheese, if desired.

Makes 8 servings

Minestrone alla Milanese

- **2 cans (about 14 ounces *each*) reduced-sodium beef broth**
- **1 can (about 14 ounces) diced tomatoes**
- **1 cup diced red potatoes**
- **1 cup coarsely chopped carrots**
- **1 cup coarsely chopped green cabbage**
- **1 cup sliced zucchini**
- **½ cup chopped onion**
- **½ cup sliced fresh green beans**
- **½ cup coarsely chopped celery**
- **½ cup water**
- **2 tablespoons olive oil**
- **1 clove garlic, minced**
- **½ teaspoon dried basil**
- **¼ teaspoon dried rosemary**
- **1 whole bay leaf**
- **1 can (about 15 ounces) cannellini beans, rinsed and drained**
   Grated Parmesan cheese (optional)

1. Combine broth, tomatoes, potatoes, carrots, cabbage, zucchini, onion, beans, celery, water, oil, garlic, basil, rosemary and bay leaf in **CROCK-POT®** slow cooker; stir to blend. Cover; cook on LOW 5 to 6 hours.

2. Add cannellini beans. Cover; cook on LOW 1 hour or until vegetables are tender.

3. Remove and discard bay leaf. Top with cheese, if desired.

Makes 8 servings

French Lentil Rice Soup

Nutrition Information

Serving Size: about
1½ cups

Calories 170
Total Fat 1g
Saturated Fat 0g
Protein 10g
Carbohydrate 28g
Cholesterol 0mg
Fiber 11g
Sodium 670mg

Dietary Exchanges:
1½ Starch, 1 Vegetable

6 cups fat-free reduced-sodium chicken or vegetable broth
1 cup dried lentils, rinsed and sorted
2 medium carrots, finely diced
1 small onion, finely chopped
2 medium stalks celery, finely diced
3 tablespoons uncooked rice
2 tablespoons minced garlic
1 teaspoon herbes de Provence or dried thyme
½ teaspoon salt
⅛ teaspoon ground white pepper or black pepper
¼ cup whipping cream or sour cream, divided (optional)
¼ cup chopped fresh parsley (optional)

1. Combine broth, lentils, carrots, onion, celery, rice, garlic, herbes de Provence, salt and pepper in **CROCK-POT**® slow cooker; stir to blend. Cover; cook on LOW 8 hours or on HIGH 4 to 5 hours.

2. Purée soup, 1 cup at a time, in food processor or blender, returning blended soup to **CROCK-POT**® slow cooker after each batch. (Or, use hand-held immersion blender.)

3. Top each serving with cream, if desired, and parsley.

Makes 6 servings

Note

To skin chicken easily,
grasp skin with paper
towel and pull away.
Repeat with fresh paper
towel for each piece of
chicken, discarding
skins and towels.

Creamy Farmhouse Chicken and Garden Soup

- **½ package (16 ounces) frozen pepper stir-fry vegetable mix**
- **1 cup frozen corn**
- **1 medium zucchini, sliced**
- **2 bone-in chicken thighs, skinned**
- **½ teaspoon minced garlic**
- **1 can (about 14 ounces) fat-free chicken broth**
- **½ teaspoon dried thyme**
- **2 ounces uncooked egg noodles**
- **1 cup fat-free half-and-half**
- **½ cup frozen peas, thawed**
- **2 tablespoons finely chopped fresh parsley**
- **2 tablespoons unsalted butter**
- **1 teaspoon salt**
- **½ teaspoon coarsely ground black pepper**

1. Coat inside of **CROCK-POT**® slow cooker with nonstick cooking spray. Place stir-fry vegetables, corn and zucchini in bottom. Add chicken, garlic, broth and thyme. Cover; cook on HIGH 3 to 4 hours or until chicken is no longer pink in center. Remove chicken; set aside to cool slightly.

2. Add noodles to **CROCK-POT**® slow cooker. Cover; cook on HIGH 20 minutes or until noodles are heated through.

3. Meanwhile, debone and chop chicken. Return to **CROCK-POT**® slow cooker. Stir in half-and-half, peas, parsley, butter, salt and pepper. Turn off heat. Let stand 5 minutes before serving.

Makes 6 servings

Rustic Vegetable Soup

1 jar (16 ounces) picante sauce
1 package (10 ounces) frozen mixed vegetables
1 package (10 ounces) frozen cut green beans
1 can (about 10 ounces) condensed beef broth, undiluted
1 to 2 baking potatoes, cut into ½-inch pieces
1 medium green bell pepper, chopped
½ teaspoon sugar
¼ cup finely chopped fresh Italian parsley

Combine picante sauce, mixed vegetables, green beans, broth, potatoes, bell pepper and sugar in **CROCK-POT®** slow cooker; stir to blend. Cover; cook on LOW 8 hours or on HIGH 4 hours. Stir in parsley just before serving.

Makes 8 servings

Cauliflower Soup

2 **heads cauliflower, cut into small florets**

8 **cups fat-free reduced-sodium vegetable broth**

¾ **cup chopped celery**

¾ **cup chopped onion**

1 **teaspoon salt**

2 **teaspoons black pepper**

2 **cups whole milk or light cream**

1 **teaspoon reduced-sodium Worcestershire sauce**

1. Combine cauliflower, broth, celery, onion, salt and pepper in **CROCK-POT®** slow cooker. Cover; cook on LOW 7 to 8 hours or on HIGH 3 to 4 hours.

2. Process soup, 1 cup at a time, in food processor or blender, returning blended soup to **CROCK-POT®** slow cooker after each batch. (Or, use hand-held immersion blender.)

3. Add milk and Worcestershire sauce to food processor or blender; process until blended. Cover; cook on HIGH 15 to 20 minutes before serving.

Makes 8 servings

Nutrition Information

Serving Size: about 1½ cups

Calories 70
Total Fat.........................2g
Saturated Fat 1g
Protein 4g
Carbohydrate 8g
Cholesterol 5mg
Fiber 2g
Sodium.................800mg

Dietary Exchanges:
1 Vegetable

Nutrition Information

Serving Size: about 1½ cups

Calories 200
Total Fat.......................6g
Saturated Fat 2g
Protein 20g
Carbohydrate 22g
Cholesterol 60mg
Fiber 6g
Sodium.................700mg

Dietary Exchanges:
1 Starch, 1 Vegetable

Mexican Chicken and Black Bean Soup

4 bone-in chicken thighs, skinned

1 can (about 15 ounces) no-salt-added black beans, rinsed and drained

1 can (about 14 ounces) fat-free reduced-sodium chicken broth

1 can (about 14 ounces) diced tomatoes with mild green chiles or diced tomatoes with Mexican seasoning

1 cup finely chopped onion

1 cup frozen corn

1 can (4 ounces) chopped mild green chiles

1 tablespoon chili powder

1 teaspoon salt

1 teaspoon ground cumin

Optional toppings: sour cream, sliced avocado, shredded cheese, chopped fresh cilantro and/or fried tortilla strips

1. Coat inside of **CROCK-POT**® slow cooker with nonstick cooking spray. Add chicken, beans, broth, tomatoes, onion, corn, chiles, chili powder, salt and cumin; stir to blend. Cover; cook on HIGH 3 to 4 hours.

2. Remove chicken to large cutting board using slotted spoon. Debone and chop chicken. Return chicken to **CROCK-POT**® slow cooker; stir well. Serve in bowls. Top as desired.

Makes 6 servings

Rich and Hearty Drumstick Soup

 2 **turkey drumsticks (about 1⅓ pounds total)**
 2 **medium carrots, sliced**
 1 **medium stalk celery, thinly sliced**
 1 **cup chopped onion**
 1 **teaspoon minced garlic**
 ½ **teaspoon poultry seasoning**
4½ **cups fat-free reduced-sodium chicken broth**
 2 **ounces uncooked dry egg noodles**
 ¼ **cup chopped fresh Italian parsley**
 1 **tablespoon unsalted butter**
 ¾ **teaspoon salt**

1. Coat inside of **CROCK-POT**® slow cooker with nonstick cooking spray. Add drumsticks, carrots, celery, onion, garlic and poultry seasoning; pour in broth. Cover; cook on HIGH 5 hours or until meat is falling off bones.

2. Remove drumsticks to large cutting board. Add noodles to **CROCK-POT**® slow cooker. Cover; cook on HIGH 30 minutes or until noodles are cooked through. Meanwhile, debone turkey, remove skin and cut meat into 1-inch pieces. Stir turkey, parsley, butter and salt into **CROCK-POT**® slow cooker just before serving.

Makes 6 servings

Greek Lemon and Rice Soup

Nutrition Information

Serving Size: 1 cup

Calories 90
Total Fat........................3g
Saturated Fat 1g
Protein 3g
Carbohydrate 14g
Cholesterol 100mg
Fiber 0g
Sodium.................500mg

Dietary Exchanges:
½ Starch, ½ Fat

Note

Soup may be served
hot or cold. To serve
cold, allow soup to cool
to room temperature.
Cover and refrigerate
up to 24 hours before
serving.

3 cans (about 14 ounces *each*) fat-free reduced-sodium chicken broth

½ cup uncooked long grain rice (not converted or instant rice)

3 egg yolks

¼ cup lemon juice

¼ teaspoon salt

⅛ teaspoon ground white pepper*

4 thin slices lemon (optional)

4 teaspoons finely chopped fresh Italian parsley (optional)

*You may substitute black pepper.

1. Combine broth and rice in **CROCK-POT**® slow cooker. Cover; cook on HIGH 2 to 3 hours or until rice is tender.

2. Turn **CROCK-POT**® slow cooker to LOW. Stir egg yolks and lemon juice in medium bowl. Stir large spoonful of hot rice mixture into egg yolk mixture. Whisk back into **CROCK-POT**® slow cooker. Cover; cook on LOW 10 minutes. Season with salt and pepper. Garnish with lemon slices and parsley.

Makes 6 servings

Country Turkey and Veggie Soup

2 tablespoons unsalted butter, divided
8 ounces sliced mushrooms
½ cup chopped onion
½ cup thinly sliced celery
1 medium red bell pepper, chopped
1 medium carrot, thinly sliced
½ teaspoon dried thyme
4 cups fat-free reduced-sodium chicken or turkey broth
4 ounces uncooked egg noodles
2 cups chopped cooked skinless turkey breast
1 cup fat-free half-and-half
½ cup frozen peas, thawed
¾ teaspoon salt

1. Melt 1 tablespoon butter in large nonstick skillet over medium-high heat. Add mushrooms and onion; cook and stir 4 minutes or until onion is translucent.

2. Remove mixture to **CROCK-POT**® slow cooker. Add celery, bell pepper, carrot and thyme; pour in broth. Cover; cook on HIGH 2½ hours.

3. Add noodles and turkey. Cover; cook on HIGH 20 minutes. Stir in half-and-half, peas, remaining 1 tablespoon butter and salt. Cover; cook on HIGH until noodles are tender and soup is heated through.

Makes 8 servings

Nutrition Information

Serving Size: about 1 cup

Calories 200
Total Fat.........................5g
Saturated Fat................1g
Protein 8g
Carbohydrate 30g
Cholesterol 0mg
Fiber 4g
Sodium.................790mg

Dietary Exchanges:
½ Starch, ½ Vegetable,
½ Milk, 1 Fat

Roasted Corn and Red Pepper Chowder

2 tablespoons extra virgin olive oil

2 cups fresh corn or frozen corn, thawed

1 medium red bell pepper, diced

2 medium green onions, sliced

4 cups fat-free reduced-sodium chicken broth

2 baking potatoes, peeled and diced

1 teaspoon salt

½ teaspoon black pepper

1 can (13 ounces) nonfat evaporated milk

2 tablespoons minced fresh Italian parsley

1. Heat oil in large skillet over medium heat. Add corn, bell pepper and green onions; cook and stir 7 to 8 minutes or until vegetables are tender and lightly browned. Remove to **CROCK-POT**® slow cooker.

2. Add broth, potatoes, salt and black pepper; stir well to combine. Cover; cook on LOW 7 to 9 hours or on HIGH 4 to 5 hours. Stir in evaporated milk 30 minutes before serving. Garnish each serving with parsley.

Makes 6 servings

Kale, Olive Oil and Parmesan Soup

Nutrition Information

Serving Size: 1 cup

Calories 140
Total Fat.........................6g
Saturated Fat................1g
Protein 7g
Carbohydrate 20g
Cholesterol 0mg
Fiber 4g
Sodium................. 670mg

Dietary Exchanges:
4 Vegetable, 1 Fat

- **8** **cups chicken broth**
- **1** **small Spanish onion, sliced**
- **3** **cloves garlic, minced**
- **2** **tablespoons olive oil**
  Kosher salt and black pepper (optional)
- **2** **pounds kale, washed and chopped**
  Grated Parmesan cheese (optional)
  Extra virgin olive oil (optional)

1. Add broth, onion, garlic, olive oil, salt and black pepper, if desired, to **CROCK-POT**® slow cooker. Cover; cook on LOW 4 hours or on HIGH 2 hours.

2. Stir in kale. Cover; cook on HIGH 15 minutes or until heated through. Spoon into individual serving bowls. If desired, sprinkle with cheese and drizzle with extra virgin olive oil, just before serving.

Makes 6 servings

Nutrition Information

Serving Size: 1 cup

Calories 130
Total Fat.......................3g
Saturated Fat 2g
Protein 3g
Carbohydrate 24g
Cholesterol 10mg
Fiber 3g
Sodium.................680mg

Dietary Exchanges:
½ Vegetable, ½ Fat

Tip

Use caution when processing hot liquids in blender. Vent lid of blender and cover with clean kitchen towel as directed by manufacturer.

Curried Sweet Potato and Carrot Soup

2 medium sweet potatoes, peeled and cut into ¾-inch pieces (about 5 cups)

4 cups fat-free chicken broth

2 cups baby carrots

1 small onion, chopped

¾ teaspoon curry powder

½ teaspoon salt

½ teaspoon black pepper

½ teaspoon ground cinnamon

¼ teaspoon ground ginger

¾ cup half-and-half

1 tablespoon maple syrup

Candied ginger (optional)

1. Combine potatoes, broth, carrots, onion, curry powder, salt, pepper, cinnamon and ground ginger in **CROCK-POT**® slow cooker; mix well. Cover; cook on LOW 7 to 8 hours.

2. Purée soup, 1 cup at a time, in food processor or blender, returning blended soup to **CROCK-POT**® slow cooker after each batch. (Or, use hand-held immersion blender.)

3. Stir in half-and-half and maple syrup. Turn **CROCK-POT**® slow cooker to HIGH. Cover; cook on HIGH 15 minutes or until heated through. Garnish with candied ginger.

Makes 8 servings

Pasta Fagioli Soup

Tip

Only small pasta varieties like tubetti, ditalini or small shell-shaped pasta should be used in this recipe. The low heat of a **CROCK-POT®** slow cooker won't allow larger pasta shapes to cook completely.

- 2 cans (about 14 ounces *each*) fat-free reduced-sodium beef or vegetable broth
- 1 can (about 15 ounces) Great Northern beans, rinsed and drained
- 1 can (about 14 ounces) diced tomatoes
- 2 medium zucchini, quartered lengthwise and sliced
- 1 tablespoon olive oil
- 1½ teaspoons minced garlic
- ½ teaspoon dried basil
- ½ teaspoon dried oregano
- ½ cup uncooked ditalini, tubetti or small shell pasta
- ½ cup garlic seasoned croutons
- ½ cup grated Asiago or Romano cheese
- 3 tablespoons chopped fresh basil or Italian parsley (optional)

1. Combine broth, beans, tomatoes, zucchini, oil, garlic, dried basil and oregano in **CROCK-POT®** slow cooker; stir to blend. Cover; cook on LOW 3 to 4 hours.

2. Stir in pasta. Cover; cook on LOW 1 hour or until pasta is tender. Serve with croutons and cheese. Garnish with fresh basil.

Makes 6 servings

Spring Pea and Mint Broth Soup

Nutrition Information

Serving Size: about
1 cup

Calories 190
Total Fat.........................1g
Saturated Fat 0g
Protein 10g
Carbohydrate 36g
Cholesterol 0mg
Fiber 11g
Sodium.................220mg

Dietary Exchanges:
1½ Starch, 2½ Vegetable

8 cups water

3 medium carrots, sliced

2 medium onions, coarsely chopped

3 leeks, cleaned well and coarsely chopped

2 stalks celery, sliced

1 bunch fresh mint

1 bag (32 ounces) frozen peas *or* 4 cups fresh spring peas

1 tablespoon fresh lemon juice

   Kosher salt and black pepper (optional)

   Creme fraîche or sour cream (optional)

1. Combine water, carrots, onions, leeks, celery and mint in **CROCK-POT**® slow cooker. Cover; cook on HIGH 5 hours.

2. Strain broth and return to **CROCK-POT**® slow cooker. Discard solids. Add peas and lemon juice. Cover; cook on LOW 4 to 5 hours or on HIGH 2 to 3 hours.

3. Season with salt and pepper, if desired. Ladle soup into bowls and garnish with dollop of creme fraîche.

Makes 8 servings

Nutrition Information

Serving Size: about
1 cup

Calories 120
Total Fat.....................4g
Saturated Fat 0g
Protein 14g
Carbohydrate 8g
Cholesterol 30mg
Fiber 1g
Sodium.................690mg

Dietary Exchanges:
½ Vegetable, 1 Meat,
½ Fat

Simmering Hot and Sour Soup

  2 **cans (about 14 ounces *each*) fat-free reduced-sodium chicken broth**
  1 **cup chopped cooked chicken or pork**
  4 **ounces fresh shiitake mushroom caps, thinly sliced**
  ½ **cup thinly sliced bamboo shoots**
  3 **tablespoons rice wine vinegar**
  2 **tablespoons reduced-sodium soy sauce**
1½ **teaspoons chili paste *or* 1 teaspoon hot chili oil**
  4 **ounces firm tofu, drained and cut into ½-inch pieces**
  2 **teaspoons sesame oil**
  2 **tablespoons cold water**
  2 **tablespoons cornstarch**
    Chopped fresh cilantro or sliced green onions (optional)

1. Combine broth, chicken, mushrooms, bamboo shoots, vinegar, soy sauce and chili paste in **CROCK-POT®** slow cooker; stir to blend. Cover; cook on LOW 3 to 4 hours or on HIGH 2 to 3 hours.

2. Stir in tofu and sesame oil. Stir water into cornstarch in small bowl until smooth; whisk into soup. Cover; cook on HIGH 10 minutes or until soup is thickened. Garnish with cilantro.

Makes 6 servings

BEEF AND LAMB MAIN DISHES

Cajun Beef Stew

1	tablespoon Cajun or blackened seasoning mix
1½	pounds cubed beef stew meat
2	medium red potatoes, unpeeled and cut into 1½-inch pieces
3	carrots, cut into 1-inch pieces
1	medium onion, cut into 1½-inch pieces
1	stalk celery, sliced
1	can (about 14 ounces) beef broth
3	tablespoons water
3	tablespoons cornstarch
1	cup frozen peas, thawed
	Sprigs fresh thyme (optional)

1. Coat inside of **CROCK-POT**® slow cooker with nonstick cooking spray. Sprinkle seasoning mix over meat in medium bowl; toss to coat. Place potatoes, carrots, onion and celery in **CROCK-POT**® slow cooker. Place beef on top of vegetables. Add broth. Cover; cook on LOW 7 to 8 hours or on HIGH 4 to 5 hours.

2. Remove beef and vegetables to large bowl using slotted spoon; cover and keep warm. Stir water into cornstarch in small bowl until smooth. Whisk into **CROCK-POT**® slow cooker. Cover; cook on HIGH 10 to 15 minutes or until thickened.

3. Return beef and vegetables to **CROCK-POT**® slow cooker. Stir in peas. Cover; cook on HIGH 15 minutes or until heated through. Garnish each serving with thyme.

Makes 4 servings

Nutrition Information

Serving Size: 1 cup

Calories	298
Total Fat	7g
Saturated Fat	2g
Protein	29g
Carbohydrate	29g
Cholesterol	55mg
Fiber	4g
Sodium	580mg

Dietary Exchanges:
2 Starch, 3 Meat

Nutrition Information

Serving Size: 1 slice
(4 ounces) roast and
about ¾ cup vegetables

Calories 250
Total Fat........................6g
Saturated Fat 2g
Protein 30g
Carbohydrate 21g
Cholesterol 55mg
Fiber 4g
Sodium................. 530mg

Dietary Exchanges:
½ Starch, 1½ Vegetable,
3½ Meat

New England Chuck Roast

- **1 lean boneless beef chuck roast (3¼ pounds), string on***
- **2 teaspoons salt**
- **¼ teaspoon black pepper**
- **2 tablespoons olive oil**
- **4 cups water, divided**
- **2 cups carrots, cut into 2-inch pieces**
- **2 medium stalks celery, cut into 1-inch pieces**
- **1½ cups yellow onion, cut into quarters**
- **4 small red potatoes, cut into quarters**
- **3 whole bay leaves**
- **2 tablespoons white vinegar**
- **2 tablespoons prepared horseradish**
- **1 head cabbage, cut into quarters or eighths**
- **4 tablespoons all-purpose flour**
- **2 tablespoons cornstarch**

Unless you have a 5-, 6- or 7-quart **CROCK-POT® slow cooker, cut any roast larger than 2½ pounds in half so it cooks completely.*

1. Season roast with salt and pepper. Heat oil in large skillet over medium heat. Brown roast on all sides, turning as it browns. Remove to **CROCK-POT**® slow cooker.

2. Add 3 cups water, carrots, celery, onion, potatoes, bay leaves, vinegar and horseradish. Cover; cook on LOW 5 to 7 hours or on HIGH 2 to 4 hours.

3. One hour before serving, add cabbage to **CROCK-POT**® slow cooker. Stir remaining 1 cup water into flour and cornstarch in small bowl until smooth. Add to **CROCK-POT**® slow cooker. Cover; cook on HIGH 1 hour or until thickened. Remove and discard bay leaves. Serve roast with sauce and vegetables.

Makes 12 servings

Texas-Style Barbecued Brisket

- 3 **tablespoons Worcestershire sauce**
- 1 **tablespoon chili powder**
- 1 **teaspoon celery salt**
- 1 **teaspoon black pepper**
- 1 **teaspoon liquid smoke**
- 2 **cloves garlic, minced**
- 1 **beef brisket (3 to 4 pounds), trimmed***
- 2 **whole bay leaves**
- 1¾ **cups Barbecue Sauce (page 83)**

*Unless you have a 5-, 6- or 7-quart **CROCK-POT**® slow cooker, cut any roast larger than 2½ pounds in half so it cooks completely.*

1. Combine Worcestershire sauce, chili powder, celery salt, pepper, liquid smoke and garlic in small bowl; stir to blend. Spread mixture on all sides of beef. Place beef in large resealable food storage bag; seal bag. Refrigerate 24 hours.

2. Place beef, marinade and bay leaves in **CROCK-POT**® slow cooker. Cover; cook on LOW 7 hours. Meanwhile, prepare Barbecue Sauce.

3. Remove beef to large cutting board. Pour cooking liquid into 2-cup measure; let stand 5 minutes. Skim off and discard fat. Remove and discard bay leaves. Stir 1 cup cooking liquid into barbecue sauce in medium bowl. Discard any remaining cooking liquid.

4. Return beef and barbecue sauce mixture to **CROCK-POT**® slow cooker. Cover; cook on LOW 1 hour or until meat is fork-tender. Remove beef to cutting board. Cut across grain into ¼-inch-thick slices. Serve with Barbecue Sauce.

Makes 10 to 12 servings

Barbecue Sauce

- **2 tablespoons vegetable oil**
- **1 onion, chopped**
- **2 cloves garlic, minced**
- **1 cup ketchup**
- **½ cup molasses**
- **¼ cup cider vinegar**
- **2 teaspoons chili powder**
- **½ teaspoon dry mustard**

1. Heat oil in medium saucepan over medium heat. Add onion and garlic; cook and stir until onion is tender.

2. Stir in ketchup, molasses, vinegar, chili powder and dry mustard; simmer over medium heat 5 minutes.

Makes about 1¾ cups

Nutrition Information

Serving Size: ½ cup

Calories 220
Total Fat......................5g
Saturated Fat 2g
Protein 28g
Carbohydrate 13g
Cholesterol 50mg
Fiber 2g
Sodium..................210mg

Dietary Exchanges:
1 Vegetable, 3½ Meat

Horseradish Roast Beef and Potatoes

- **1 tablespoon freshly grated horseradish**
- **1 tablespoon Dijon mustard**
- **1 tablespoon minced fresh Italian parsley**
- **1 teaspoon dried thyme, basil or oregano**
- **3 pounds lean beef roast***
- **1 to 2 pounds Yukon Gold potatoes, peeled and quartered**
- **1 pound mushrooms, chopped**
- **2 cans (about 10 ounces *each*) fat-free reduced-sodium beef broth**
- **2 large tomatoes, seeded and diced**
- **1 large onion, sliced**
- **1 green bell pepper, chopped**
- **1 red bell pepper, chopped**
- **1 cup dry red wine**
- **3 cloves garlic, minced**
- **1 whole bay leaf**

*Unless you have a 5-, 6- or 7-quart **CROCK-POT**® slow cooker, cut any roast larger than 2½ pounds in half so it cooks completely.*

1. Combine horseradish, mustard, parsley and thyme in small bowl. Place roast in **CROCK-POT**® slow cooker and spread paste over roast.

2. Add potatoes, mushrooms, broth, tomatoes, onion, bell peppers, wine, garlic and bay leaf to **CROCK-POT**® slow cooker. Add enough water to cover roast and vegetables. Cover; cook on HIGH 2 hours. Turn **CROCK-POT**® slow cooker to LOW. Cover; cook on LOW 4 to 6 hours. Remove and discard bay leaf. Shred beef into 1-inch pieces before serving.

Makes 12 servings

Merlot'd Beef and Sun-Dried Tomato Portobello Ragoût

Nutrition Information

Serving Size: 1¼ cups

Calories 260
Total Fat 11g
Saturated Fat 3g
Protein 29g
Carbohydrate 10g
Cholesterol 65mg
Fiber 2g
Sodium................. 350mg

Dietary Exchanges:
1½ Vegetable, ½ Fat

1 jar (7 ounces) sun-dried tomatoes in oil, drained, 3 tablespoons oil reserved

1 lean boneless chuck roast (about 2¾ pounds), cut into 1½-inch pieces

1 can (about 14 ounces) fat-free reduced-sodium beef broth

6 ounces sliced portobello mushrooms

1 medium green bell pepper, cut into thin strips

1 medium orange or yellow bell pepper, cut into thin strips

1 medium onion, cut into 8 wedges

2 teaspoons dried oregano

½ teaspoon salt, plus additional for seasoning

¼ teaspoon garlic powder

½ cup Merlot or other dry red wine

2 tablespoons Worcestershire sauce

1 tablespoon balsamic vinegar

1 tablespoon cornstarch

Black pepper (optional)

Mashed potatoes, rice or egg noodles (optional)

1. Heat 1 tablespoon reserved oil in large skillet over medium-high heat. Add ⅓ of beef; brown on all sides. Remove to **CROCK-POT®** slow cooker. Repeat with remaining reserved oil and beef.

2. Add broth to skillet; cook and stir, scraping up any browned bits from skillet. Pour mixture over beef. Add sun-dried tomatoes, mushrooms, bell peppers, onion, oregano, ½ teaspoon salt and garlic powder to **CROCK-POT®** slow cooker.

3. Combine Merlot and Worcestershire sauce in small bowl; reserve ¼ cup. Gently stir remaining Merlot mixture into **CROCK-POT®** slow cooker. Cover; cook on LOW 8 to 9 hours or on HIGH 4 to 5 hours or until beef is tender.

4. Stir vinegar and cornstarch into reserved ¼ cup Merlot mixture until cornstarch is dissolved. Add to **CROCK-POT**® slow cooker; stir until well blended. Cover; cook on HIGH 15 minutes or until thickened slightly. Season with additional salt and black pepper, if desired. Serve over mashed potatoes, if desired.

Makes 10 servings

Tip

CROCK-POT® slow cookers cook at a low heat for a long time, so they are a great way to cook dishes calling for less tender cuts of meat. Long, slow cooking helps tenderize these cuts of meat.

Beef with Apples and Sweet Potatoes

1 lean boneless beef chuck shoulder roast (about 2 pounds)
1 can (40 ounces) sweet potatoes, drained
2 small onions, sliced
2 medium apples, cored and sliced
½ cup fat-free reduced-sodium beef broth
2 cloves garlic, minced
1 teaspoon salt
1 teaspoon dried thyme, divided
¾ teaspoon black pepper, divided
2 tablespoons cold water
1 tablespoon cornstarch
¼ teaspoon ground cinnamon

1. Trim excess fat from beef and discard. Cut beef into 2-inch pieces. Place beef, potatoes, onions, apples, broth, garlic, salt, ½ teaspoon thyme and ½ teaspoon pepper in **CROCK-POT®** slow cooker. Cover; cook on LOW 8 to 9 hours.

2. Turn off heat. Remove beef, potatoes, onions and apples to large serving platter; cover with foil to keep warm. Let cooking liquid stand 5 minutes to allow fat to rise. Skim off and discard fat.

3. Stir water into cornstarch, remaining ½ teaspoon thyme, ¼ teaspoon pepper and cinnamon in small bowl until smooth; whisk into cooking liquid. Turn **CROCK-POT®** slow cooker to HIGH. Cover; cook on HIGH 15 minutes or until cooking liquid is thickened. Serve sauce over beef, potatoes, onions and apples.

Makes 8 servings

Nutrition Information

Serving Size:
about 4 meatballs,
1 cup sauce and spinach,
⅓ cup noodles

Calories	278
Total Fat	5g
Saturated Fat	2g
Protein	22g
Carbohydrate	34g
Cholesterol	38mg
Fiber	3g
Sodium	295mg

Dietary Exchanges:
2 Starch, 2 Meat

Greek-Style Meatballs and Spinach

½ **cup old-fashioned oats**

¼ **cup minced onion**

1 **clove garlic, minced**

¼ **teaspoon dried oregano**

⅛ **teaspoon black pepper**

¼ **cup cholesterol-free egg substitute**

8 **ounces lean ground lamb**

1 **cup reduced-sodium beef broth**

¼ **teaspoon salt**

½ **cup plain nonfat yogurt**

1 **teaspoon all-purpose flour**

4 **cups fresh baby spinach, coarsely chopped**

1⅓ **cups hot cooked no-yolk egg noodles**

1. Combine oats, onion, garlic, oregano and pepper in medium bowl. Stir in egg substitute. Add lamb; mix well but do not knead. Shape mixture into 16 balls. Place in **CROCK-POT**® slow cooker. Add broth and salt. Cover; cook on LOW 6 hours.

2. Stir yogurt into flour in small bowl. Spoon about ¼ cup hot liquid from **CROCK-POT**® slow cooker into yogurt mixture; stir until smooth. Whisk yogurt mixture into **CROCK-POT**® slow cooker. Add spinach. Cover; cook on LOW 10 minutes or until heated through. Serve over noodles.

Makes 4 servings

Nutrition Information

Serving Size: 1 slice (3 ounces) meat with about ¾ cup vegetables

Calories	296
Total Fat	8g
Saturated Fat	3g
Protein	28g
Carbohydrate	25g
Cholesterol	57mg
Fiber	4g
Sodium	381mg

Dietary Exchanges:
½ Starch, 3 Vegetable,
½ Fruit, 3 Meat

Sauerbraten

- **1 boneless beef rump roast (1¼ pounds)**
- **3 cups baby carrots**
- **1½ cups fresh or frozen pearl onions**
- **¼ cup raisins**
- **½ cup water**
- **½ cup red wine vinegar**
- **1 tablespoon honey**
- **½ teaspoon salt**
- **½ teaspoon dry mustard**
- **½ teaspoon garlic-pepper seasoning**
- **¼ teaspoon ground cloves**
- **¼ cup crushed crisp gingersnap cookies (5 cookies)**

1. Heat large nonstick skillet over medium-high heat. Brown roast on all sides, turning as it browns. Place roast, carrots, onions and raisins in **CROCK-POT®** slow cooker.

2. Combine water, vinegar, honey, salt, dry mustard, garlic-pepper seasoning and cloves in small bowl; mix well. Pour mixture over meat and vegetables in **CROCK-POT®** slow cooker. Cover; cook on LOW 4 to 6 hours.

3. Remove roast to large cutting board. Cover loosely with foil; let stand 10 to 15 minutes before slicing. Remove vegetables from **CROCK-POT®** slow cooker to large bowl using slotted spoon; cover to keep warm.

4. Stir crushed cookies into sauce mixture in **CROCK-POT®** slow cooker. Turn **CROCK-POT®** slow cooker to HIGH. Cover; cook on HIGH 10 to 15 minutes or until sauce thickens. Serve meat and vegetables with sauce.

Makes 5 servings

Tip

Cooking times for **CROCK-POT®** slow cookers, just like ovens, cook differently depending on a variety of factors. For example, cooking times will be longer at higher altitudes.

Slow Cooker Pepper Steak

    2 tablespoons vegetable oil
    2¾ pounds lean boneless beef top sirloin steak, cut into strips (boneless chuck roast)
    5 to 6 cloves garlic, minced
    1 medium onion, chopped
    ½ cup reduced-sodium soy sauce
    2 teaspoons sugar
    1 teaspoon salt
    ½ teaspoon ground ginger
    ½ teaspoon black pepper
    3 green bell peppers, cut into strips
    ¼ cup cold water
    1 tablespoon cornstarch
       Hot cooked rice (optional)

1. Heat oil in large skillet over medium-low heat. Brown steak strips in two batches. Add garlic; cook and stir 2 minutes. Remove steak strips, garlic and pan juices to **CROCK-POT®** slow cooker.

2. Add onion, soy sauce, sugar, salt, ginger and black pepper to **CROCK-POT®** slow cooker; mix well. Cover; cook on LOW 6 to 8 hours or until meat is tender (up to 10 hours). Add bell pepper strips during final hour of cooking.

3. Stir water into cornstarch in small bowl until smooth; whisk into **CROCK-POT®** slow cooker. Turn **CROCK-POT®** slow cooker to HIGH. Cook, uncovered, on HIGH 15 minutes or until thickened. Serve with rice, if desired.

Makes 10 servings

Stuffed Baby Bell Peppers

- **1 tablespoon olive oil**
- **½ onion, chopped**
- **½ pound ground beef**
- **½ cup cooked rice**
- **3 tablespoons chopped fresh Italian parsley**
- **2 tablespoons lemon juice**
- **1 tablespoon dried dill weed**
- **1 tablespoon tomato paste, divided**
- **½ teaspoon salt**
- **⅛ teaspoon black pepper**
- **¼ cup fat-free reduced-sodium beef broth**
- **1 bag yellow and red baby bell peppers (about 2 dozen)**

1. Heat oil in medium skillet over medium heat. Add onion; cook and stir 5 minutes or until translucent.

2. Add beef; brown 6 to 8 minutes, stirring to break up meat. Drain fat. Remove to large bowl. Add rice, parsley, lemon juice, dill, 1½ teaspoons tomato paste, salt and black pepper; mix well. Whisk broth and remaining 1½ teaspoons tomato paste in small bowl.

3. Cut lengthwise slit down side of each bell pepper; run under cold water to wash out seeds. Fill each bell pepper with 2 to 3 teaspoons meat mixture. Place filled bell peppers in **CROCK-POT**® slow cooker, filling side up. Add broth mixture. Cover; cook on LOW 5 hours or on HIGH 2½ hours.

Makes 6 servings

Nutrition Information

Serving Size: 1 slice
(4 ounces)

Calories 190
Total Fat.........................7g
Saturated Fat 3g
Protein 23g
Carbohydrate 7g
Cholesterol 80mg
Fiber 1g
Sodium................. 380mg

Dietary Exchanges:
½ Vegetable, 2½ Meat

That's Italian Meat Loaf

1 **can (8 ounces) tomato sauce, divided**
1 **egg, lightly beaten**
½ **cup chopped onion**
½ **cup chopped green bell pepper**
⅓ **cup seasoned dry bread crumbs**
2 **tablespoons grated Parmesan cheese**
½ **teaspoon garlic powder**
¼ **teaspoon black pepper**
1 **pound ground beef**
½ **pound ground pork**
1 **cup grated Asiago cheese**

1. Reserve ⅓ cup tomato sauce; refrigerate. Combine remaining tomato sauce and egg in large bowl. Stir in onion, bell pepper, bread crumbs, Parmesan cheese, garlic powder and black pepper. Add ground beef and pork; mix well and shape into loaf. Carefully remove meat loaf to **CROCK-POT®** slow cooker. Cover; cook on LOW 8 to 10 hours or on HIGH 4 to 6 hours.

2. Spread meat loaf with reserved tomato sauce; sprinkle with Asiago cheese. Cover; cook on HIGH 15 minutes or until cheese is melted.

Makes 8 servings

Tip

CROCK-POT® slow cooker recipes calling for raw meats should cook a minimum of 3 hours on LOW for food safety reasons. When in doubt, use an instant-read thermometer to ensure the meat has reached the recommended internal temperature for safe consumption.

Slow Cooker Steak Fajitas

1 lean beef flank steak (about 1 pound)
1 medium onion, cut into strips
½ cup medium salsa, plus additional for garnish
2 tablespoons chopped fresh cilantro
2 tablespoons fresh lime juice
2 cloves garlic, minced
1 tablespoon chili powder
1 teaspoon ground cumin
½ teaspoon salt
1 small green bell pepper, cut into strips
1 small red bell pepper, cut into strips
8 flour tortillas, warmed

1. Cut flank steak lengthwise in half, then crosswise into thin strips; place meat in **CROCK-POT**® slow cooker. Combine onion, ½ cup salsa, cilantro, lime juice, garlic, chili powder, cumin and salt in **CROCK-POT**® slow cooker. Cover; cook on LOW 5 to 6 hours.

2. Add bell peppers. Cover; cook on LOW 1 hour.

3. Serve with flour tortillas and additional salsa, if desired.

Makes 4 servings

Barbecued Meatballs

Nutrition Information

Serving Size:
3 meatballs

Calories 170
Total Fat.......................3g
Saturated Fat...............2g
Protein 13g
Carbohydrate 23g
Cholesterol 45mg
Fiber 1g
Sodium.................600mg

Dietary Exchanges:
1 Starch, ½ Vegetable,
2 Meat

- 2 pounds 95% lean ground beef
- 1⅓ cups ketchup, divided
- 3 tablespoons seasoned dry bread crumbs
- 1 egg, lightly beaten
- 2 tablespoons dried minced onion
- ¾ teaspoon garlic salt
- ½ teaspoon black pepper
- 1 cup packed brown sugar
- 1 can (6 ounces) tomato paste
- ¼ cup reduced-sodium soy sauce
- ¼ cup cider vinegar
- 1½ teaspoons hot pepper sauce
- Sliced green bell peppers (optional)

1. Preheat oven to 350°F. Combine beef, ⅓ cup ketchup, bread crumbs, egg, dried onion, garlic salt and black pepper in medium bowl; mix lightly but thoroughly. Shape into 1-inch meatballs.

2. Place meatballs in two 15×10-inch jelly-roll pans or shallow roasting pans. Bake 18 minutes or until browned. Remove to **CROCK-POT**® slow cooker using slotted spoon.

3. Mix remaining 1 cup ketchup, brown sugar, tomato paste, soy sauce, vinegar and hot pepper sauce in medium bowl. Pour over meatballs. Cover; cook on LOW 4 hours. Stir in bell peppers during last 15 minutes of cooking, if desired.

Makes 12 servings

Hungarian Lamb Goulash

- **1 package (16 ounces) frozen cut green beans, thawed**
- **1 cup chopped onion**
- **1¼ pounds lean lamb for stew, cut into 1-inch cubes**
- **1 can (15 ounces) chunky tomato sauce**
- **1½ cups fat-free reduced-sodium chicken broth**
- **1 can (6 ounces) tomato paste**
- **4 teaspoons paprika**
- **3 cups hot cooked egg noodles**

1. Place green beans and onion in **CROCK-POT®** slow cooker. Top with lamb.

2. Combine tomato sauce, broth, tomato paste and paprika in large bowl; mix well. Pour over lamb mixture. Cover; cook on LOW 6 to 8 hours. Stir goulash; serve over noodles.

Makes 6 servings

Tavern Burger

- **2 pounds 95% lean ground beef**
- **½ cup ketchup**
- **¼ cup packed brown sugar**
- **¼ cup yellow mustard**
- **8 hamburger buns**

1. Brown beef in large skillet over medium-high heat 6 to 8 minutes, stirring to break up meat. Drain fat. Remove beef to **CROCK-POT**® slow cooker.

2. Add ketchup, brown sugar and mustard to **CROCK-POT**® slow cooker; mix well. Cover; cook on LOW 4 to 6 hours. Serve on buns.

Makes 8 servings

Nutrition Information

Serving Size: 1 burger

Calories 200
Total Fat........................ 6g
Saturated Fat............... 3g
Protein 25g
Carbohydrate 11g
Cholesterol 70mg
Fiber 0g
Sodium................. 330mg

Dietary Exchanges:
½ Starch, 3½ Meat

Tip

This recipe is also known to some people as "BBQs" or "loose-meat sandwiches." For additional flavor, add a can of pork and beans when adding the other ingredients.

Niku Jaga (Japanese Beef Stew)

Nutrition Information

Serving Size: 1 cup

Calories 230
Total Fat 8g
Saturated Fat 3g
Protein 22g
Carbohydrate 16g
Cholesterol 50mg
Fiber 2g
Sodium 510mg

Dietary Exchanges:
½ Vegetable, 3 Meat,
½ Fat

- **2 tablespoons vegetable oil**
- **2 pounds cubed beef stew meat**
- **4 medium carrots, diagonally sliced**
- **3 medium Yukon Gold potatoes, peeled and chopped**
- **1 medium white onion, peeled and chopped**
- **1 cup water**
- **½ cup Japanese sake or dry white wine**
- **¼ cup sugar**
- **¼ cup reduced-sodium soy sauce**
- **1 teaspoon salt**

1. Heat oil in large skillet over medium heat. Brown beef on all sides, turning as it browns. Remove beef to **CROCK-POT®** slow cooker.

2. Add carrots, potatoes, onion, water, sake, sugar, soy sauce and salt; stir to blend. Cover; cook on LOW 10 to 12 hours or on HIGH 4 to 6 hours.

Makes 10 servings

Nutrition Information

Serving Size: 1 cup

Calories 212
Total Fat 8g
Saturated Fat 3g
Protein 15g
Carbohydrate 17g
Cholesterol 32mg
Fiber 6g
Sodium................. 290mg

Dietary Exchanges:
2 Starch, 2 Vegetable

Chili Mac

1 **pound ground beef**
½ **cup chopped onion**
1 **can (about 14 ounces) diced tomatoes, drained**
1 **can (8 ounces) tomato sauce**
2 **tablespoons chili powder**
1 **teaspoon garlic salt**
½ **teaspoon ground cumin**
¼ **teaspoon red pepper flakes**
¼ **teaspoon black pepper**
8 **ounces uncooked elbow macaroni**
Shredded Cheddar cheese (optional)

1. Brown beef and onion in large skillet over medium heat 6 to 8 minutes, stirring to break up meat. Drain fat. Remove beef mixture to **CROCK-POT**® slow cooker.

2. Add tomatoes, tomato sauce, chili powder, garlic salt, cumin, red pepper flakes and black pepper; mix well. Cover; cook on LOW 4 hours.

3. Cook macaroni according to package directions until al dente; drain. Add macaroni to **CROCK-POT**® slow cooker; mix well. Cover; cook on LOW 1 hour. Garnish with cheese.

Makes 6 servings

Beef Stew with Bacon, Onion and Sweet Potatoes

1 **pound cubed beef stew meat**

1 **can (about 14 ounces) beef broth**

2 **medium sweet potatoes, cut into 2-inch pieces**

1 **large onion, chopped**

2 **slices thick-cut bacon, diced**

1 **teaspoon dried thyme**

1 **teaspoon salt**

¼ **teaspoon black pepper**

2 **tablespoons water**

2 **tablespoons cornstarch**

1. Coat inside of **CROCK-POT®** slow cooker with nonstick cooking spray. Combine beef, broth, potatoes, onion, bacon, thyme, salt and pepper in **CROCK-POT®** slow cooker; stir to blend.

2. Cover; cook on LOW 7 to 8 hours or on HIGH 4 to 5 hours or until beef and vegetables are tender. Remove beef and vegetables to serving bowl using slotted spoon. Cover and keep warm.

3. Stir water into cornstarch in small bowl until smooth; whisk into **CROCK-POT®** slow cooker. Cover; cook on LOW 15 minutes or until thickened. Serve sauce evenly over beef and vegetables.

Makes 4 servings

Dilly Beef Sandwiches

1 lean boneless beef chuck roast (2¾ pounds), cut into 1-inch pieces*

1 jar (6 ounces) sliced dill pickles, undrained

1 can (about 14 ounces) crushed tomatoes with Italian seasoning

1 medium onion, diced

4 cloves garlic, minced

1 teaspoon mustard seeds

Hamburger buns, toasted

Optional toppings: lettuce, sliced tomatoes and/or sliced red onions

Unless you have a 5-, 6- or 7-quart **CROCK-POT® slow cooker, cut any roast larger than 2½ pounds in half so it cooks completely.*

1. Place beef in **CROCK-POT**® slow cooker. Pour pickles with juice over beef. Add crushed tomatoes, onion, garlic and mustard seeds. Cover; cook on LOW 8 to 10 hours.

2. Remove beef to large cutting board; shred with two forks. Return beef to tomato mixture; mix well. Serve on toasted buns. Top as desired.

Makes 10 servings

Lamb and Vegetable Stew

2 cups sliced mushrooms

1 large red bell pepper, diced

1 large carrot, cut into ½-inch-thick slices

1 large leek, white part only, chopped

1 small new potato, unpeeled and diced

1 small parsnip, cut into ½-inch-thick slices

1 clove garlic, minced

½ cup reduced-sodium beef broth

½ teaspoon dried thyme

¼ teaspoon dried rosemary

⅛ teaspoon black pepper

12 ounces lamb shoulder meat, cut into 1-inch pieces

2 tablespoons all-purpose flour

½ teaspoon salt (optional)

1. Place mushrooms, bell pepper, carrot, leek, potato, parsnip and garlic in **CROCK-POT**® slow cooker. Add broth, thyme, rosemary and black pepper; stir. Add lamb. Cover; cook on LOW 6 to 7 hours.

2. Stir 2 tablespoons liquid from **CROCK-POT**® slow cooker into flour in small bowl until smooth. Stir flour mixture into **CROCK-POT**® slow cooker. Turn **CROCK-POT**® slow cooker to HIGH. Cover; cook on HIGH 10 minutes. Season with salt, if desired.

Makes 4 servings

Tip

This chunky chili is
perfect for the spicy
food lover in your family.
Reduce red pepper
flakes for a milder flavor.

Kick'n Chili

2 pounds 95% lean ground beef
1 tablespoon ground cumin
1 tablespoon dried oregano
1 tablespoon chili powder
1 tablespoon paprika
1 tablespoon black pepper
2 cloves garlic, minced
2 teaspoons red pepper flakes
1½ teaspoons salt
¼ teaspoon ground red pepper
1 tablespoon vegetable oil
3 cans (10½ ounces *each*) diced tomatoes with mild green chiles
1 jar (16 ounces) salsa
1 medium onion, chopped
8 yellow bell peppers, seeded and tops sliced off (optional)

1. Combine beef, cumin, oregano, chili powder, paprika, black pepper, garlic, red pepper flakes, salt and ground red pepper in large bowl.

2. Heat oil in large skillet over medium-high heat. Add beef; cook and stir 6 to 8 minutes or until browned. Remove beef mixture to **CROCK-POT®** slow cooker using slotted spoon. Add tomatoes, salsa and onion; stir to blend. Cover; cook on LOW 4 to 6 hours. Serve chili in bell peppers, if desired.

Makes 8 servings

Shredded Beef Wraps

Nutrition Information

Serving Size: 1 wrap

Calories 280
Total Fat.......................9g
Saturated Fat...............3g
Protein 28g
Carbohydrate 21g
Cholesterol 35mg
Fiber 1g
Sodium.................540mg

Dietary Exchanges:
1 Starch, 1 Vegetable,
3½ Meat

1 lean beef flank steak or beef skirt steak (1 to 1½ pounds), cut into 4 equal pieces

1 cup fat-free reduced-sodium beef broth

½ cup sun-dried tomatoes (not packed in oil), chopped

3 to 4 cloves garlic, minced

¼ teaspoon ground cumin

4 (8-inch) flour tortillas

Optional toppings: shredded lettuce, diced tomatoes and/or shredded Monterey Jack cheese

1. Combine beef, broth, sun-dried tomatoes, garlic and cumin in **CROCK-POT**® slow cooker. Cover; cook on LOW 7 to 8 hours or until meat is tender.

2. Remove beef to large cutting board; shred with two forks. Place remaining contents from **CROCK-POT**® slow cooker in blender or food processor; blend until smooth.

3. Spoon beef and sauce evenly onto tortillas. Top as desired. Roll up to serve.

Makes 4 servings

PORK MAIN DISHES

Pork and Mushroom Ragoût

Nonstick cooking spray

1 **boneless pork loin roast (1¼ pounds)**

1¼ **cups canned crushed tomatoes, divided**

2 **tablespoons cornstarch**

2 **teaspoons dried savory**

3 **sun-dried tomatoes (not packed in oil), chopped**

1 **package (8 ounces) sliced mushrooms**

1 **large onion, sliced**

1 **teaspoon black pepper**

3 **cups hot cooked noodles**

1. Spray large skillet with cooking spray; heat skillet over medium heat. Brown roast on all sides; set aside.

2. Place ½ cup tomatoes, cornstarch, savory and sun-dried tomatoes in **CROCK-POT**® slow cooker; mix well. Layer mushrooms, onion and pork over tomato mixture.

3. Pour remaining ¾ cup tomatoes over pork; sprinkle with pepper. Cover; cook on LOW 4 to 6 hours.

4. Remove roast to large cutting board. Cover loosely with foil; let stand 10 to 15 minutes before slicing. Serve with sauce over noodles.

Makes 6 servings

Nutrition Information

Serving Size: 1 slice (3 ounces) pork with ½ cup sauce and ½ cup noodles

Calories 275
Total Fat........................7g
Saturated Fat 2g
Protein 21g
Carbohydrate 33g
Cholesterol 68mg
Fiber 3g
Sodium..................169mg

Dietary Exchanges:
2 Starch, 1 Vegetable, 2 Meat

121

Pork Roast with Currant Cherry Salsa

1½ teaspoons chili powder

¾ teaspoon salt

½ teaspoon garlic powder

½ teaspoon paprika

¼ teaspoon ground allspice

1 boneless pork loin roast (2 pounds)
Nonstick cooking spray

½ cup water

1 package (1 pound) frozen pitted dark cherries, thawed, drained and halved

¼ cup currants or dark raisins

1 teaspoon grated orange peel

1 teaspoon balsamic vinegar

⅛ to ¼ teaspoon red pepper flakes

1. Combine chili powder, salt, garlic powder, paprika and allspice in small bowl. Rub roast evenly with spice mixture, pressing spices into roast.

2. Spray large skillet with cooking spray; heat over medium-high heat. Brown roast on all sides. Place in **CROCK-POT**® slow cooker.

3. Pour water into skillet, stirring to scrape up brown bits. Pour liquid into **CROCK-POT**® slow cooker. Cover; cook on LOW 6 to 8 hours.

4. Remove roast to large cutting board. Cover loosely with foil; let stand 10 to 15 minutes. Strain juice from **CROCK-POT**® slow cooker; discard solids. Pour juice into small saucepan; keep warm over low heat.

5. Turn **CROCK-POT**® slow cooker to HIGH. Add cherries, currants, orange peel, vinegar and red pepper flakes to **CROCK-POT**® slow cooker. Cover; cook on HIGH 30 minutes. Slice pork; spoon warm juice over meat. Serve with salsa.

Makes 8 servings

Nutrition Information

Serving Size: 1 pork cutlet with ¼ of onion gravy

Calories 200
Total Fat.........................6g
Saturated Fat...............2g
Protein 26g
Carbohydrate 7g
Cholesterol 70mg
Fiber 1g
Sodium................. 520mg

Dietary Exchanges:
1 Fruit, 3 Meat

Peppered Pork Cutlets with Onion Gravy

½ **teaspoon paprika**

¼ **teaspoon ground cumin**

¼ **teaspoon black pepper**

4 **boneless pork cutlets (4 ounces *each*)**

Nonstick cooking spray

2 **cups thinly sliced onions**

2 **tablespoons all-purpose flour, divided**

¾ **cup water**

1½ **teaspoons chicken bouillon granules**

2 **tablespoons fat-free (skim) milk**

¼ **teaspoon salt**

1. Combine paprika, cumin and black pepper in small bowl; blend well. Sprinkle spice mixture evenly over one side of each cutlet, pressing down gently to adhere. If time allows, let stand 15 minutes to absorb flavors.

2. Spray large skillet with cooking spray; heat skillet over medium heat. Add pork, seasoned side down; cook 3 minutes or until browned. Remove to **CROCK-POT**® slow cooker.

3. Increase heat to medium-high; spray skillet with additional cooking spray. Add onions to skillet; cook and stir 4 minutes or until browned. Sprinkle with 1½ tablespoons flour; toss to coat. Add water and bouillon; stir to blend and bring to a boil. Add onions and any accumulated juices to **CROCK-POT**® slow cooker, spooning some of the sauce over pork. Cover; cook on LOW 4 to 5 hours.

4. Place pork on warm serving platter; set aside. Turn **CROCK-POT**® slow cooker to HIGH. Stir milk into remaining ½ tablespoon flour in small bowl; whisk into **CROCK-POT**® slow cooker. Add salt. Cover; cook on HIGH 10 minutes or until thickened. Spoon sauce over pork.

Makes 4 servings

Nutrition Information

Serving Size: 1 pork chop with about ½ cup apple-cherry glaze

Calories 243
Total Fat 8g
Saturated Fat 3g
Protein 19g
Carbohydrate 23g
Cholesterol 40mg
Fiber 1g
Sodium.................... 191mg

Dietary Exchanges:
1½ Fruit, 2 Meat, 1 Fat

Apple-Cherry Glazed Pork Chops

½ to 1 teaspoon dried thyme

¼ teaspoon salt

¼ teaspoon black pepper

4 boneless pork loin chops (3 ounces *each*), trimmed
   Nonstick olive oil cooking spray

1⅓ cups unsweetened apple juice

1 small apple, unpeeled and sliced

¼ cup sliced green onions

¼ cup dried tart cherries

2 tablespoons water

2 teaspoons cornstarch

1. Combine thyme, salt and pepper in small bowl. Rub onto both sides of pork chops. Spray large skillet with cooking spray; heat over medium-high heat. Working in batches, brown pork on both sides. Remove to **CROCK-POT®** slow cooker.

2. Add apple juice, apple slices, green onions and cherries to same skillet. Simmer, uncovered, 2 to 3 minutes or until apple and onions are tender. Stir water into cornstarch in small bowl until smooth; whisk into skillet. Bring to a boil; cook and stir until thickened. Spoon over pork chops.

3. Cover; cook on LOW 3½ to 4 hours or until pork chops are tender. To serve, spoon fruit and cooking liquid over pork chops.

Makes 4 servings

Spiced Pork and Apple Stew

1	teaspoon canola oil
1¼	pounds cubed lean pork stew meat
1	medium sweet onion, cut into ½-inch-thick slices
2	cloves garlic, minced
1	can (28 ounces) crushed tomatoes
2	large or 3 small red or white potatoes, cut into 1-inch pieces
1½	cups baby carrots, cut into ½-inch pieces
2	small apples, cored and cubed
1	cup reduced-sodium chicken broth
2	tablespoons spicy brown mustard
1	tablespoon packed brown sugar
2	teaspoons ground cinnamon
1	teaspoon ground cumin
¼	teaspoon salt
2	tablespoons chopped fresh Italian parsley (optional)

1. Heat oil in large skillet over medium-high heat. Add pork; brown on all sides. Add onion and garlic; cook and stir 5 minutes. Remove to **CROCK-POT**® slow cooker.

2. Add tomatoes, potatoes, carrots, apples, broth, mustard, brown sugar, cinnamon, cumin and salt to **CROCK-POT**® slow cooker. Cover; cook on LOW 6 to 8 hours or until pork and potatoes are tender. Garnish with parsley.

Makes 8 servings

Cherry & Mushroom Stuffed Pork Chops

2 **tablespoons vegetable oil, divided**
1 **cup chopped shiitake mushrooms**
¼ **cup finely chopped onion**
¼ **cup finely chopped celery**
¼ **cup dried sweetened cherries, chopped**
¼ **teaspoon salt**
⅛ **teaspoon dried thyme**
⅛ **teaspoon black pepper**
4 **boneless pork loin chops (about 1¼ pounds), cut 1 inch thick**
1 **teaspoon all-purpose flour**
¼ **cup fat-free reduced-sodium chicken broth**
¼ **cup cherry juice**

1. Heat 1 tablespoon oil in large skillet over medium-high heat. Add mushrooms, onion and celery; cook and stir over medium-high heat 4 minutes. Stir in cherries, salt, thyme and pepper. Remove mixture to small bowl; set aside.

2. Brown pork chops in same skillet 2 minutes on both sides over medium-high heat. Cook in two batches, if necessary. Remove pork from skillet. Pour off fat. Add flour to skillet; cook 30 seconds, stirring constantly. Stir in broth and juice, scraping up any browned bits from bottom of skillet. Cook 1 minute to thicken sauce slightly.

3. Make deep pocket in side of each pork chop; fill each with one fourth of cherry stuffing. Skewer pockets closed with toothpicks. Arrange pork chops in **CROCK-POT**® slow cooker, pocket side up. Pour sauce from skillet evenly over pork chops. Cover; cook on LOW 4 to 5 hours or until pork chops are tender. Remove toothpicks before serving.

Makes 4 servings

Barbecued Pulled Pork Sandwiches

Nutrition Information

Serving Size: 1 sandwich

Calories 480
Total Fat...................... 13g
Saturated Fat 3g
Protein 30g
Carbohydrate 58g
Cholesterol 75mg
Fiber 3g
Sodium................. 740mg

Dietary Exchanges:
1 Starch, 2½ Meat, 1 Fat

Tip

For a 5-, 6- or 7-quart **CROCK-POT®** slow cooker, double all ingredients, except for the barbecue sauce. Increase the barbecue sauce to 1½ bottles (about 21 ounces total).

1 pork top loin roast (2½ pounds)
1 bottle (14 ounces) barbecue sauce
1 medium onion, chopped
10 sesame seed buns

1. Place pork roast in **CROCK-POT®** slow cooker. Cover; cook on LOW 10 to 12 hours or on HIGH 5 to 6 hours.

2. Remove pork to large cutting board; shred with two forks. Discard cooking liquid. Return shredded pork to **CROCK-POT®** slow cooker. Stir in barbecue sauce and onion. Cover; cook on LOW 2 hours or on HIGH 1 hour. Serve on rolls.

Makes 10 servings

Simple Shredded Pork Tacos

1¾ pounds lean boneless pork loin roast

1 cup salsa

1 can (4 ounces) chopped mild green chiles

½ teaspoon garlic salt

½ teaspoon black pepper

6 (8-inch) corn tortillas

Optional toppings: sour cream, diced tomatoes or sliced jalapeño peppers

1. Place roast, salsa, chiles, garlic salt and pepper in **CROCK-POT®** slow cooker. Cover; cook on LOW 8 hours.

2. Remove pork to large cutting board; shred with two forks. Spoon shredded pork evenly into tortillas with sauce. Top as desired.

Makes 6 servings

Nutrition Information

Serving Size: 1 taco

Calories 190
Total Fat........................4g
Saturated Fat 2g
Protein 30g
Carbohydrate 4g
Cholesterol 75mg
Fiber 1g
Sodium................ 370mg

Dietary Exchanges:
1 Starch, 1 Fat

Tip

Cut the pork roast to fit in the bottom of your **CROCK-POT®** slow cooker in one or two layers.

Tip

To reduce the amount of fat in **CROCK-POT®** slow cooker meals, trim excess fat from meats and degrease canned broth before using.

Jerk Pork and Sweet Potato Stew

- 3 tablespoons all-purpose flour
- ¼ teaspoon salt
- ¼ teaspoon black pepper
- 1¼ pounds lean pork shoulder, cut into 1-inch pieces
- 2 tablespoons vegetable oil
- 1 large sweet potato, diced
- 1 cup frozen or canned corn
- ¼ cup minced green onions (green parts only), divided
- 1 clove garlic, minced
- 1 medium jalapeño pepper or Scotch bonnet chile, cored, seeded and minced (about 1 teaspoon)*
- ⅛ teaspoon ground allspice
- 1 cup fat-free reduced-sodium chicken broth
- 1 tablespoon lime juice
- 2 cups cooked rice (optional)

*Jalapeño peppers and Scotch bonnet chiles can sting and irritate the skin, so wear rubber gloves when handling and do not touch your eyes.

1. Combine flour, salt and black pepper in large resealable food storage bag. Add pork; shake well to coat. Heat oil in large skillet over medium heat. Add pork in single layer (working in two batches, if necessary) and brown on both sides, about 5 minutes. Remove to **CROCK-POT®** slow cooker.

2. Add sweet potato, corn, 2 tablespoons green onions, garlic, jalapeño pepper and allspice. Stir in broth. Cover; cook on LOW 5 to 6 hours.

3. Stir in lime juice and remaining 2 tablespoons green onions. Serve stew with rice, if desired.

Makes 6 servings

Serving Size: 1 (½-inch) slice

Calories 190
Total Fat 10g
Saturated Fat 3g
Protein 21g
Carbohydrate 18g
Cholesterol 57mg
Fiber 1g
Sodium 184mg

Dietary Exchanges:
1 Starch, 2½ Meat

Apple Stuffed Pork Loin Roast

1 **tablespoon butter**

2 **large tart apples, peeled, cored and thinly sliced (about 2 cups)**

1 **medium onion, cut into thin strips (about 1 cup)**

2 **tablespoons packed brown sugar**

1 **teaspoon Dijon mustard**

2 **cloves garlic, minced**

1 **teaspoon coarse salt**

1 **teaspoon dried rosemary**

½ **teaspoon dried thyme**

½ **teaspoon black pepper**

1 **boneless center cut pork loin roast (4 to 5 pounds)***

1 **cup apple cider or apple juice**

Unless you have a 5-, 6- or 7-quart **CROCK-POT® slow cooker, cut any roast larger than 2½ pounds in half so it cooks completely.*

1. Melt butter in large skillet over medium-high heat. Add apples and onion; cook and stir 5 minutes or until soft. Stir in brown sugar and mustard. Set aside.

2. Combine garlic, salt, rosemary, thyme and pepper in small bowl. Cut lengthwise down roast almost to, but not through, bottom. Open like a book. Rub half of garlic mixture onto cut sides of pork.

3. Spread apple mixture evenly onto one cut side of roast. Close halves; tie roast with kitchen string at 2-inch intervals.

4. Coat inside of **CROCK-POT**® slow cooker with nonstick cooking spray. Place roast in **CROCK-POT**® slow cooker. Pour apple cider over roast. Rub outside of roast with remaining garlic mixture. Cover; cook on LOW 5 to 6 hours or on HIGH 2 to 3 hours or until roast is tender.

5. Remove roast to large cutting board. Cover loosely with foil; let stand 10 to 15 minutes. Slice roast just before serving.

Makes 16 servings

Tip

If your pepper mill doesn't produce a coarse grind, you can place whole peppercorns in a small resealable food storage bag. Use a rolling pin to crush and grind them neatly.

Spicy Citrus Pork with Pineapple Salsa

- 1 **tablespoon ground cumin**
- 1 **teaspoon black pepper**
- ½ **teaspoon salt**
- 3 **pounds lean boneless center-cut pork loin, rinsed and patted dry***
- 2 **tablespoons vegetable oil**
- 4 **cans (8 ounces *each*) pineapple tidbits in own juice, drained and ½ cup juice reserved****
- 3 **tablespoons lemon juice, divided**
- 1 **cup finely chopped orange or red bell pepper**
- ¼ **cup finely chopped red onion**
- 2 **tablespoons chopped fresh cilantro or mint**
- 2 **teaspoons grated lemon peel**

*Unless you have a 5-, 6- or 7-quart **CROCK-POT**® slow cooker, cut any roast larger than 2½ pounds in half so it cooks completely.*

**If tidbits are unavailable, purchase pineapple chunks and coarsely chop.*

1. Coat inside of **CROCK-POT**® slow cooker with nonstick cooking spray. Combine cumin, black pepper and salt in small bowl. Rub evenly onto pork. Heat oil in medium skillet over medium heat. Brown pork on all sides, 1 to 2 minutes per side. Remove to **CROCK-POT**® slow cooker.

2. Spoon 4 tablespoons of reserved pineapple juice and 2 tablespoons lemon juice over pork. Cover; cook on LOW 2 to 2¼ hours or on HIGH 1 hour and 10 minutes or until meat is tender.

3. Meanwhile, combine pineapple, remaining 4 tablespoons pineapple juice, remaining 1 tablespoon lemon juice, bell pepper, onion, cilantro and lemon peel in medium bowl. Toss gently; set aside.

4. Remove pork to large serving platter. Let pork stand 10 minutes before slicing into six pieces. Arrange pork slices on large serving platter. To serve, pour sauce evenly over slices. Serve with salsa.

Makes 6 servings

Pork Roast with Dijon Tarragon Glaze

1½ **to 2 pounds boneless pork loin, trimmed**
   1 **teaspoon ground paprika**
   ½ **teaspoon black pepper**
   ⅓ **cup reduced-sodium chicken or vegetable broth**
   2 **tablespoons Dijon mustard**
   2 **tablespoons lemon juice**
   1 **teaspoon minced fresh tarragon**

1. Sprinkle pork with paprika and pepper. Place roast in **CROCK-POT®** slow cooker. Combine broth, mustard, lemon juice and tarragon in small bowl; spoon over pork.

2. Cover; cook on LOW 6 to 8 hours or on HIGH 3 to 4 hours. Remove roast to large cutting board. Cover loosely with foil; let stand 10 to 15 minutes before slicing. Serve with cooking liquid.

Makes 6 servings

Stew Provençal

- **2 cans (about 14 ounces *each*) fat-free reduced-sodium beef broth, divided**
- **⅓ cup all-purpose flour**
- **1 to 2 lean pork tenderloins (about 2 pounds), trimmed and diced**
- **4 medium red potatoes, unpeeled and cut into cubes**
- **2 cups frozen cut green beans, thawed**
- **1 medium onion, chopped**
- **2 cloves garlic, minced**
- **1 teaspoon salt**
- **1 teaspoon dried thyme**
- **½ teaspoon black pepper**

1. Combine ¾ cup broth and flour in small bowl. Cover and refrigerate.

2. Add remaining broth, pork, potatoes, beans, onion, garlic, salt, thyme and pepper to **CROCK-POT**® slow cooker; mix well. Cover; cook on LOW 8 to 10 hours or on HIGH 4 to 5 hours.

3. Stir flour mixture into **CROCK-POT**® slow cooker. Cook, uncovered, on HIGH 30 minutes or until thickened.

Makes 8 servings

Rough-Cut Smoky Red Pork Roast

1 **can (about 14 ounces) stewed tomatoes, drained**

1 **can (6 ounces) tomato paste with basil, oregano and garlic**

1 **cup chopped red bell pepper**

2 **to 3 canned chipotle peppers in adobo sauce, finely chopped and mashed with fork***

1 **teaspoon salt**

1 **lean pork shoulder roast (about 3¼ pounds)****

1½ **to 2 tablespoons sugar**

*For less heat, remove seeds from chipotle peppers before mashing.

***Unless you have a 5-, 6- or 7-quart **CROCK-POT**® slow cooker, cut any roast larger than 2½ pounds in half so it cooks completely.*

1. Coat inside of **CROCK-POT**® slow cooker with nonstick cooking spray.

2. Combine stewed tomatoes, tomato paste, bell pepper, chipotle peppers and salt in **CROCK-POT**® slow cooker. Add pork, fat side up. Cover; cook on HIGH 5 hours.

3. Remove pork to large cutting board. Cover loosely with foil; let stand 10 to 15 minutes. Stir sugar into cooking liquid. Cook, uncovered, on HIGH 15 minutes. To serve, remove fat from pork and slice evenly into ten pieces. Pour sauce evenly over pork slices.

Makes 10 servings

Pork Tenderloin with Cabbage

 3 cups shredded red cabbage
 ¼ cup chopped onion
 ¼ cup reduced-sodium chicken broth
 1 clove garlic, minced
 1½ pounds pork tenderloin
 ¾ cup apple juice concentrate
 3 tablespoons honey mustard
 1½ tablespoons Worcestershire sauce

1. Add cabbage, onion, broth and garlic to **CROCK-POT®** slow cooker. Place pork over cabbage mixture. Combine apple juice concentrate, mustard and Worcestershire sauce in small bowl; stir to blend. Pour over pork. Cover; cook on LOW 6 to 8 hours or on HIGH 3 to 4 hours.

2. Remove pork to large cutting board; cover loosely with foil. Let stand 10 to 15 minutes before slicing. Serve pork with cabbage and cooking liquid.

Makes 6 servings

Ham and Potato Hash

1½ **pounds red potatoes, peeled and sliced**

8 **ounces thinly sliced lean ham**

2 **poblano chile peppers, cut into thin strips**

2 **tablespoons olive oil**

1 **tablespoon dried oregano**

¼ **teaspoon salt**

1 **cup (4 ounces) shredded reduced-fat Monterey Jack or pepper jack cheese**

2 **tablespoons finely chopped fresh cilantro**

1. Combine potatoes, ham, peppers, oil, oregano and salt in **CROCK-POT®** slow cooker; mix well. Cover; cook on LOW 7 hours or on HIGH 4 hours.

2. Remove potato mixture to serving dish; sprinkle with cheese and cilantro. Let stand 3 minutes or until cheese is melted.

Makes 6 servings

Nutrition Information

Serving Size: ⅙ of total recipe

Calories 190
Total Fat 8g
Saturated Fat 3g
Protein 12g
Carbohydrate 18g
Cholesterol 25mg
Fiber 2g
Sodium................. 570mg

Dietary Exchanges:
1 Starch, 1½ Meat, 1 Fat

Nutrition Information

Serving Size: ¼ of total recipe

Calories	220
Total Fat	5g
Saturated Fat	2g
Protein	24g
Carbohydrate	15g
Cholesterol	75mg
Fiber	1g
Sodium	540mg

Dietary Exchanges:
1 Vegetable, 3 Meat

Asian Pork Tenderloin

½ cup bottled garlic ginger sauce

¼ cup sliced green onions

1 pork tenderloin (about 1 pound)

1 large red onion, cut into slices

1 medium red bell pepper, cut into 1-inch pieces

1 medium zucchini, cut into ¼-inch slices

1 tablespoon olive oil

1. Combine ginger sauce and green onions in large resealable food storage bag; add pork. Seal bag; turn to coat. Place bag in large baking pan; refrigerate 30 minutes or overnight.

2. Combine red onion, bell pepper, zucchini and oil in large bowl; toss to coat. Place vegetables in **CROCK-POT**® slow cooker. Remove pork from bag; place on top of vegetables. Discard marinade. Cover; cook on LOW 6 to 7 hours or on HIGH 4 to 5 hours.

3. Remove pork to large cutting board. Cover loosely with foil; let stand 10 to 15 minutes before slicing. Serve pork with vegetables.

Makes 4 servings

Nutrition Information

Serving Size: ¹⁄₁₀ of total recipe

Calories 210
Total Fat......................4g
Saturated Fat..............2g
Protein 29g
Carbohydrate 14g
Cholesterol 70mg
Fiber 3g
Sodium................. 720mg

Dietary Exchanges:
1 Vegetable, 3 Meat

Heavenly Harvest Pork Roast

¼ **cup pomegranate juice**

¼ **cup sugar**

1 **teaspoon salt**

1 **tablespoon garlic salt**

1 **tablespoon steak seasoning**

1 **teaspoon black pepper**

1 **lean pork loin roast (2¾ pounds)***

2 **pears, cored, peeled and sliced thick**

2 **oranges with peel, sliced thick**

*Unless you have a 5-, 6- or 7-quart **CROCK-POT**® slow cooker, cut any roast larger than 2½ pounds in half so it cooks completely.*

1. Combine pomegranate juice and sugar in small saucepan; cook and stir 2 minutes or until sugar dissolves. Pour into **CROCK-POT**® slow cooker.

2. Blend salt, garlic salt, steak seasoning and pepper in small bowl. Rub mixture over roast. Place roast in **CROCK-POT**® slow cooker. Turn roast to cover with juice mixture.

3. Top roast with pear and orange slices. Cover; cook on HIGH 6 to 8 hours or until tender. Serve with juice and fruit slices.

Makes 10 servings

Chili Verde

Nonstick cooking spray

¾ **pound boneless lean pork, cut into 1-inch cubes**

1 **pound fresh tomatillos, husks removed, rinsed and coarsely chopped**

1 **can (about 15 ounces) Great Northern beans, rinsed and drained**

1 **can (about 14 ounces) fat-free reduced-sodium chicken broth**

1 **large onion, halved and thinly sliced**

1 **can (4 ounces) diced mild green chiles**

6 **cloves garlic, sliced**

1 **teaspoon ground cumin**

Salt and black pepper (optional)

½ **cup lightly packed fresh cilantro, chopped**

1. Spray large skillet with cooking spray; heat over medium-high heat. Add pork; cook and stir 5 to 7 minutes or until browned on all sides.

2. Combine pork, tomatillos, beans, broth, onion, chiles, garlic and cumin in **CROCK-POT**® slow cooker. Cover; cook on HIGH 3 to 4 hours.

3. Season with salt and pepper, if desired. Turn **CROCK-POT**® slow cooker to LOW. Stir in cilantro. Cover; cook on LOW 10 minutes.

Makes 4 servings

Simple Slow Cooker Pork Roast

- **4 to 5 medium red potatoes, halved**
- **4 medium carrots, cut into 1-inch pieces**
- **1 marinated lean pork loin roast (2¾ pounds)***
- **½ cup water**
- **1 package (10 ounces) frozen baby peas**
- **Salt and black pepper (optional)**

If marinated roast is unavailable, prepare marinade by mixing ¼ cup olive oil, 1 tablespoon minced garlic and 1½ tablespoons Italian seasoning in small bowl. Place in large resealable food storage bag with pork roast. Marinate in refrigerator 2 hours or overnight. Unless you have a 5-, 6- or 7-quart **CROCK-POT® slow cooker, cut any roast larger than 2½ pounds in half so it cooks completely.*

Place potatoes, carrots and pork roast in **CROCK-POT**® slow cooker. Add water. Cover; cook on LOW 6 to 8 hours or until vegetables are tender. Add peas during last hour of cooking. Remove pork to large serving platter. Season with salt and pepper, if desired. Slice evenly into ten slices and serve with vegetables.

Makes 10 servings

Pork in Chile Sauce

- 2 **cups no-salt-added tomato purée**
- 2 **large tomatoes, chopped**
- 2 **small poblano peppers, seeded and chopped**
- 2 **large shallots *or* 1 small onion, chopped**
- 2 **cloves garlic, minced**
- ½ **teaspoon dried oregano**
- ¼ **teaspoon chipotle chili powder or regular chili powder***
- ¼ **teaspoon black pepper**
- 2 **boneless pork chops (6 ounces *each*), cut into 1-inch pieces**
- ½ **teaspoon salt (optional)**
- 4 **whole wheat or corn tortillas, warmed (optional)**

*Chipotle chili powder is available in the spice section of most supermarkets.

Place tomato purée, tomatoes, poblano peppers, shallots, garlic, oregano, chili powder and black pepper in **CROCK-POT**® slow cooker; mix well. Add pork. Cover; cook on LOW 5 to 6 hours. Stir in salt, if desired. Serve in tortillas, if desired.

Makes 4 servings

Nutrition Information

Serving Size: 1¼ cups

Calories 217
Total Fat 7g
Saturated Fat 2g
Protein 22g
Carbohydrate 20g
Cholesterol 54mg
Fiber 3g
Sodium 89mg

Dietary Exchanges:
1 Starch, 3 Meat

155

Nutrition Information

Serving Size: ¼ of pork mixture with ⅓ cup cooked rice

Calories 313
Total Fat 6g
Saturated Fat 2g
Protein 21g
Carbohydrate 42g
Cholesterol 49mg
Fiber 4g
Sodium 406mg

Dietary Exchanges:
2 Starch, 2 Vegetable, 2 Meat

Orange Teriyaki Pork

Nonstick cooking spray
1 pound cubed lean pork stew meat
1 package (16 ounces) frozen bell pepper blend for stir-fry
4 ounces sliced water chestnuts
½ cup orange juice
2 tablespoons quick-cooking tapioca
2 tablespoons packed brown sugar
2 tablespoons teriyaki sauce
½ teaspoon ground ginger
½ teaspoon dry mustard
1⅓ cups hot cooked rice

1. Spray large skillet with cooking spray; heat skillet over medium heat. Add pork; brown on all sides. Remove from heat; set aside.

2. Place bell peppers and water chestnuts in **CROCK-POT®** slow cooker. Top with browned pork. Mix orange juice, tapioca, brown sugar, teriyaki sauce, ginger and dry mustard in large bowl. Pour juice mixture over pork in **CROCK-POT®** slow cooker. Cover; cook on LOW 3 to 4 hours. Serve with rice.

Makes 4 servings

Spicy Asian Pork Bundles

 1 **lean boneless pork loin roast (about 3 pounds)***
 ½ **cup reduced-sodium soy sauce**
 1 **tablespoon chili paste or chili garlic sauce**
 2 **teaspoons minced fresh ginger**
 2 **tablespoons water**
 1 **tablespoon cornstarch**
 2 **teaspoons dark sesame oil**
 1 **cup shredded carrots**
 10 **large romaine lettuce leaves**

Unless you have a 5-, 6- or 7-quart **CROCK-POT® slow cooker, cut any roast larger than 2½ pounds in half so it cooks completely.*

1. Combine pork, soy sauce, chili paste and ginger in **CROCK-POT**® slow cooker; stir to blend. Cover; cook on LOW 8 to 10 hours.

2. Turn off heat. Remove roast to large cutting board. Trim and discard excess fat. Shred pork with two forks. Skim off and discard fat from cooking liquid.

3. Stir water, cornstarch and sesame oil in small bowl until smooth; whisk into cooking liquid. Turn **CROCK-POT**® slow cooker to HIGH. Cook, uncovered, on HIGH 15 minutes or until thickened.

4. Return pork to **CROCK-POT**® slow cooker; stir in carrots. Cover; cook on HIGH 15 to 30 minutes or until heated through. Spoon about ¼ cup pork filling evenly onto lettuce leaves. Wrap to enclose.

Makes 5 servings

White Bean Chili

Nonstick cooking spray

1 pound ground chicken

3 cups coarsely chopped celery

1 can (28 ounces) whole tomatoes, undrained and coarsely chopped

1 can (about 15 ounces) Great Northern beans, rinsed and drained

1½ cups coarsely chopped onions

1 cup chicken broth

3 cloves garlic, minced

4 teaspoons chili powder

1½ teaspoons ground cumin

¾ teaspoon ground allspice

¾ teaspoon ground cinnamon

½ teaspoon black pepper

1. Spray large skillet with cooking spray; heat over medium-high heat. Add chicken; cook 6 to 8 minutes or until browned, stirring to break up meat.

2. Combine chicken, celery, tomatoes, beans, onions, broth, garlic, chili powder, cumin, allspice, cinnamon and pepper in **CROCK-POT®** slow cooker. Cover; cook on LOW 5½ to 6 hours.

Makes 6 servings

Nutrition Information

Serving Size: ⅙ of total recipe

Calories 148
Total Fat........................2g
Saturated Fat 1g
Protein 15g
Carbohydrate 21g
Cholesterol 26mg
Fiber 7g
Sodium..................657mg

Dietary Exchanges:
1 Starch, 1 Vegetable, 1 Meat

Mini Meatball Grinders

1 **can (about 14 ounces) diced tomatoes, drained and juices reserved**

1 **can (8 ounces) no-salt-added tomato sauce**

¼ **cup chopped onion**

2 **tablespoons tomato paste**

1 **teaspoon Italian seasoning**

1 **pound ground chicken**

½ **cup fresh whole wheat or white bread crumbs (1 slice bread)**

1 **egg white, lightly beaten**

3 **tablespoons finely chopped fresh Italian parsley**

2 **cloves garlic, minced**

⅛ **teaspoon black pepper**

Nonstick cooking spray

4 **hard rolls, split and toasted**

3 **tablespoons grated Parmesan cheese (optional)**

1. Combine tomatoes, ½ cup reserved juice, tomato sauce, onion, tomato paste and Italian seasoning in **CROCK-POT®** slow cooker. Cover; cook on LOW 3 to 4 hours.

2. Prepare meatballs halfway through cooking time. Combine chicken, bread crumbs, egg white, parsley, garlic and pepper in medium bowl; mix well. Shape mixture into 12 meatballs. Cover; refrigerate 30 minutes.

3. Spray medium skillet with cooking spray; heat over medium heat. Add meatballs; cook 8 to 10 minutes or until well browned on all sides. Remove meatballs to **CROCK-POT®** slow cooker using slotted spoon. Cover; cook on LOW 1 to 2 hours or until no longer pink in center.

4. Place 3 meatballs in each roll; top with sauce. Sprinkle with cheese, if desired. Cut each roll into thirds.

Makes 4 servings

Nutrition Information

Serving Size: 1 filled pita halve

Calories	250
Total Fat	8g
Saturated Fat	3g
Protein	19g
Carbohydrate	24g
Cholesterol	45mg
Fiber	2g
Sodium	780mg

Dietary Exchanges:
1 Starch, ½ Vegetable, 2 Meat, 1 Fat

Greek Chicken Pitas with Creamy Mustard Sauce

Filling

- **1 medium green bell pepper, sliced into ½-inch strips**
- **1 medium onion, cut into 8 wedges**
- **½ pound boneless, skinless chicken breasts, rinsed and patted dry**
- **1 tablespoon extra virgin olive oil**
- **2 teaspoons Greek seasoning**
- **¼ teaspoon salt**

Sauce

- **¼ cup nonfat plain yogurt**
- **¼ cup fat-free mayonnaise**
- **1 tablespoon prepared mustard**
- **4 whole pita bread rounds, halved**
- **½ cup reduced-fat crumbled feta cheese**

  Optional toppings: sliced cucumbers, sliced tomatoes and/or kalamata olives

1. Coat inside of **CROCK-POT®** slow cooker with nonstick cooking spray. Place bell pepper and onion in bottom. Add chicken; drizzle with oil. Sprinkle evenly with Greek seasoning and salt. Cover; cook on HIGH 1¾ hours or until chicken is no longer pink in center and vegetables are crisp-tender.

2. Whisk yogurt, mayonnaise and mustard in small bowl until smooth. Remove chicken to large cutting board; slice. Remove vegetables using slotted spoon. Fill pita halves evenly with chicken, yogurt sauce, vegetables and feta cheese. Top as desired.

Makes 8 servings

Indian-Style Apricot Chicken

Serving Size: 1 chicken thigh with about ½ cup sauce

Calories 210
Total Fat........................5g
Saturated Fat................1g
Protein 15g
Carbohydrate 26g
Cholesterol 65mg
Fiber 4g
Sodium.................400mg

Dietary Exchanges:
1 Vegetable, 1½ Fruit, ½ Fat

- **6 skinless chicken thighs, rinsed and patted dry (about 2 pounds)**
- **¼ teaspoon salt**
- **¼ teaspoon black pepper**
- **1 tablespoon vegetable oil**
- **1 large onion, chopped**
- **2 cloves garlic, minced**
- **2 tablespoons grated fresh ginger**
- **½ teaspoon ground cinnamon**
- **⅛ teaspoon ground allspice**
- **1 can (about 14 ounces) diced tomatoes**
- **1 cup fat-free reduced-sodium chicken broth**
- **½ package (4 ounces) dried apricots**
- **Pinch saffron threads (optional)**
- **Hot cooked rice (optional)**
- **2 tablespoons chopped fresh Italian parsley (optional)**

1. Coat inside of **CROCK-POT**® slow cooker with nonstick cooking spray. Season chicken with salt and pepper. Heat oil in large skillet over medium-high heat. Add chicken; cook 6 to 8 minutes or until browned on all sides. Remove to **CROCK-POT**® slow cooker using slotted spoon.

2. Add onion to skillet; cook and stir 3 to 5 minutes or until softened. Stir in garlic, ginger, cinnamon and allspice; cook and stir 15 to 30 seconds or until mixture is fragrant. Add tomatoes and broth; cook 2 to 3 minutes or until mixture is heated through. Pour into **CROCK-POT**® slow cooker.

3. Add apricots and saffron, if desired. Cover; cook on LOW 5 to 6 hours or on HIGH 3 to 4 hours. Serve with rice, if desired. Garnish with parsley.

Makes 6 servings

Turkey Stroganoff

Nutrition Information

Serving Size: 1 cup turkey mixture with ⅓ cup noodles

Calories 313
Total Fat 3g
Saturated Fat 1g
Protein 30g
Carbohydrate 41g
Cholesterol 100mg
Fiber 3g
Sodium 123mg

Dietary Exchanges:
2 Starch, 3 Meat

Nonstick cooking spray

4 cups sliced mushrooms

2 stalks celery, thinly sliced

2 medium shallots *or* ½ small onion, minced

1 cup reduced-sodium chicken broth

½ teaspoon dried thyme

¼ teaspoon black pepper

2 turkey tenderloins, turkey breasts *or* boneless, skinless chicken thighs (about 10 ounces *each*), cut into 1-inch pieces

½ cup fat-free sour cream

1 tablespoon plus 1 teaspoon all-purpose flour

¼ teaspoon salt (optional)

1⅓ cups hot cooked wide egg noodles

1. Spray large skillet with cooking spray; heat over medium heat. Add mushrooms, celery and shallots; cook and stir 5 minutes or until mushrooms and shallots are tender. Spoon into **CROCK-POT**® slow cooker. Stir broth, thyme and pepper into **CROCK-POT**® slow cooker. Stir in turkey. Cover; cook on LOW 5 to 6 hours.

2. Mix sour cream into flour in small bowl. Spoon 2 tablespoons liquid from **CROCK-POT**® slow cooker into sour cream mixture; stir well. Stir sour cream mixture into **CROCK-POT**® slow cooker. Cover; cook on LOW 10 minutes.

3. Season with salt, if desired. Spoon noodles onto each plate to serve. Top with turkey mixture.

Makes 4 servings

Nutrition Information

Serving Size: 1 cup

Calories 342
Total Fat....................... 11g
Saturated Fat 2g
Protein 23g
Carbohydrate 32g
Cholesterol 94mg
Fiber 2g
Sodium................. 105mg

Dietary Exchanges:
2 Starch, 1 Vegetable,
3 Meat

Tip

Don't peek!
The **CROCK-POT®**
slow cooker can take as
long as 30 minutes to
regain heat lost when
the cover is removed.
Only remove the cover
when instructed to do so
by the recipe.

Moroccan Chicken Stew

1 **pound boneless, skinless chicken thighs, cut into 2-inch pieces**

½ **cup chopped celery**

½ **cup chopped carrots**

2 **ounces chopped prunes**

½ to ¾ **cup dry white wine**

⅓ **cup white balsamic vinegar**

¼ **cup packed brown sugar**

2 **tablespoons olive oil**

3 **cloves garlic, minced**

3 **whole bay leaves**

½ **teaspoon ground cinnamon**

½ **teaspoon ground coriander**

¼ **teaspoon dried oregano**

Pinch black pepper

Pinch ground ginger

Combine chicken, celery, carrots, prunes, wine, vinegar, brown sugar, oil, garlic, bay leaves, cinnamon, coriander, oregano, pepper and ginger in **CROCK-POT®** slow cooker; stir to blend. Cover; cook on LOW 3 to 4 hours. Remove and discard bay leaves.

Makes 4 servings

Turkey Meatballs in Cranberry-Barbecue Sauce

1 **can (16 ounces) jellied cranberry sauce**
½ **cup barbecue sauce**
1 **egg white**
1 **pound 93% lean ground turkey**
1 **green onion, sliced**
2 **teaspoons grated orange peel**
1 **teaspoon reduced-sodium soy sauce**
¼ **teaspoon black pepper**
⅛ **teaspoon ground red pepper (optional)**
Nonstick cooking spray

1. Combine cranberry sauce and barbecue sauce in **CROCK-POT**® slow cooker. Cover; cook on HIGH 20 to 30 minutes or until cranberry sauce melts and mixture is heated through.

2. Meanwhile, place egg white in large bowl; beat lightly. Add turkey, green onion, orange peel, soy sauce, black pepper and ground red pepper, if desired; mix until well blended. Shape into 24 meatballs.

3. Spray large skillet with cooking spray. Add meatballs; cook over medium heat 8 to 10 minutes or until meatballs are browned. Add to **CROCK-POT**® slow cooker; stir gently to coat.

4. Turn **CROCK-POT**® slow cooker to LOW. Cover; cook on LOW 3 hours.

Makes 6 servings

Autumn Chicken

1 **can (14 ounces) whole artichoke hearts, drained**
1 **can (14 ounces) whole mushrooms**
12 **boneless, skinless chicken breasts**
1 **jar (6½ ounces) marinated artichoke hearts, undrained**
¾ **cup dry white wine**
½ **cup balsamic vinaigrette**
Hot cooked noodles (optional)
Paprika (optional)

Spread whole artichokes on bottom of **CROCK-POT®** slow cooker. Top with half of mushrooms. Layer chicken over mushrooms. Add marinated artichoke hearts with liquid. Add remaining mushrooms. Pour in wine and vinaigrette. Cover; cook on LOW 4 to 5 hours. Serve over noodles, if desired. Garnish with paprika.

Makes 12 servings

Hoisin Barbecue Chicken Sliders

- ⅔ **cup hoisin sauce**
- ⅓ **cup barbecue sauce**
- 3 **tablespoons quick-cooking tapioca**
- 1 **tablespoon sugar**
- 1 **tablespoon soy sauce**
- ¼ **teaspoon red pepper flakes**
- 12 **boneless, skinless chicken thighs (3 to 3½ pounds total)**
- 16 **dinner rolls or Hawaiian sweet rolls, split**
- ½ **medium red onion, finely chopped (optional)**
  Sliced pickles (optional)

1. Combine hoisin sauce, barbecue sauce, tapioca, sugar, soy sauce and red pepper flakes in **CROCK-POT®** slow cooker; mix well. Add chicken. Cover; cook on LOW 8 to 9 hours.

2. Remove chicken to large cutting board; shred with two forks. Return shredded chicken (and any sauce that accumulates on cutting board) to **CROCK-POT®** slow cooker; stir well. Spoon ¼ cup chicken and sauce onto bottom roll. Top each with chopped onion and pickles, if desired, and top roll.

Makes 16 sliders

Nutrition Information

Serving Size: 1 slider

Calories 280
Total Fat........................8g
Saturated Fat...............3g
Protein 22g
Carbohydrate............35g
Cholesterol 75mg
Fiber 1g
Sodium.................500mg

Dietary Exchanges:
2½ Starch

Chicken Goulash

2 **small onions, chopped**

2 **stalks celery, chopped**

2 **medium carrots, chopped**

1 **clove garlic, minced**

1 **cup reduced-sodium chicken broth**

1 **cup no-salt-added tomato purée**

2 **teaspoons paprika**

½ **teaspoon dried marjoram or oregano**

¼ **teaspoon black pepper**

10 **ounces boneless, skinless chicken thighs, trimmed and cut into 1-inch pieces (2 large or 4 small thighs)**

2 **small unpeeled new potatoes, diced**

2 **teaspoons all-purpose flour**

½ **teaspoon salt (optional)**

1. Place onions, celery, carrots and garlic in **CROCK-POT**® slow cooker. Combine broth, tomato purée, paprika, marjoram and pepper in small bowl; pour over vegetables. Add chicken and potatoes to **CROCK-POT**® slow cooker. Cover; cook on LOW 5 to 6 hours.

2. Stir 2 tablespoons cooking liquid from **CROCK-POT**® slow cooker into flour in small bowl until smooth. Whisk flour mixture into **CROCK-POT**® slow cooker. Turn **CROCK-POT**® slow cooker to HIGH. Cover; cook on HIGH 10 minutes. Season with salt, if desired.

Makes 4 servings

Sweet Chicken Curry

Serving Size: 1 cup curry with ¼ cup rice

Calories 350
Total Fat 4g
Saturated Fat 1g
Protein 28g
Carbohydrate 20g
Cholesterol 85mg
Fiber 2g
Sodium 910mg

Dietary Exchanges:
1 Starch, 1 Vegetable,
1 Fruit, 3 Meat

- **1 pound boneless, skinless chicken breasts, cut into 1-inch pieces**
- **1 large green or red bell pepper, cut into 1-inch pieces**
- **1 large onion, sliced**
- **1 large tomato, seeded and chopped**
- **½ cup prepared mango chutney**
- **¼ cup water**
- **2 tablespoons cornstarch**
- **1½ teaspoons curry powder**
- **1 cup hot cooked rice**

1. Combine chicken, bell pepper and onion in **CROCK-POT®** slow cooker. Top with tomato.

2. Combine chutney, water, cornstarch and curry powder in small bowl; pour over chicken in **CROCK-POT®** slow cooker. Cover; cook on LOW 3½ to 4½ hours or until chicken is tender. Serve over rice.

Makes 4 servings

Turkey Vegetable Chili Mac

Nutrition Information

Serving Size: 1 cup

Calories 210
Total Fat.........................4g
Saturated Fat 2g
Protein 20g
Carbohydrate 24g
Cholesterol 30mg
Fiber 5g
Sodium.................340mg

Dietary Exchanges:
1 Starch, 1½ Vegetable,
1½ Meat, ½ Fat

Nonstick cooking spray

¾ **pound ground turkey**

1 **can (about 15 ounces) reduced-sodium black beans, rinsed and drained**

1 **can (about 14 ounces) Mexican-style diced tomatoes**

1 **can (about 14 ounces) no-salt-added diced tomatoes**

1 **cup frozen corn**

½ **cup chopped onion**

2 **cloves garlic, minced**

1 **teaspoon Mexican seasoning**

½ **cup (2 ounces) uncooked elbow macaroni**

⅓ **cup sour cream**

Chopped fresh Italian parsley (optional)

Cornbread (optional)

1. Spray large skillet with cooking spray; heat over medium heat. Add turkey; cook until browned. Remove to **CROCK-POT**® slow cooker with slotted spoon. Add beans, tomatoes, corn, onion, garlic and Mexican seasoning. Cover; cook on LOW 4 to 5 hours.

2. Stir in macaroni. Cover; cook on LOW 10 minutes. Stir. Cover; cook on LOW 20 to 30 minutes or until pasta is tender. Top evenly with sour cream and parsley, if desired. Serve with cornbread, if desired.

Makes 6 servings

Boneless Chicken Cacciatore

Nutrition Information

Serving Size: 1 chicken breast with ⅙ of sauce

Calories 170
Total Fat 5g
Saturated Fat 1g
Protein 20g
Carbohydrate 11g
Cholesterol 55mg
Fiber 2g
Sodium 570mg

Dietary Exchanges:
1 Starch, ½ Vegetable,
2 Meat, ½ Fat

1 tablespoon olive oil

6 boneless, skinless chicken breasts, sliced in half horizontally

4 cups reduced-sodium tomato-basil or marinara pasta sauce

1 cup coarsely chopped yellow onion

1 cup coarsely chopped green bell pepper

1 can (6 ounces) sliced mushrooms

¼ cup dry red wine (optional)

2 teaspoons minced garlic

2 teaspoons dried oregano

2 teaspoons dried thyme

1 teaspoon salt

2 teaspoons black pepper

Hot cooked pasta (optional)

1. Heat oil in large skillet over medium heat. Brown chicken breasts on both sides. Remove to **CROCK-POT**® slow cooker using slotted spoon.

2. Add pasta sauce, onion, bell pepper, mushrooms, wine, if desired, garlic, oregano, thyme, salt and black pepper to **CROCK-POT**® slow cooker; stir to blend. Cover; cook on LOW 5 to 7 hours or on HIGH 2 to 3 hours. Serve over pasta, if desired.

Makes 6 servings

Nutrition Information

Serving Size: 8 ounces of turkey with ⅓ cup sauce

Calories 203
Total Fat 1g
Saturated Fat 1g
Protein 36g
Carbohydrate 10g
Cholesterol 99mg
Fiber 1g
Sodium....................70mg

Dietary Exchanges:
½ Vegetable, ½ Fruit, 4½ Meat

Herbed Turkey Breast with Orange Sauce

1 **large onion, chopped**
3 **cloves garlic, minced**
1 **teaspoon dried rosemary**
½ **teaspoon black pepper**
1 **boneless, skinless turkey breast (3 pounds)***
1½ **cups orange juice**
Hot cooked rice (optional)

*Unless you have a 5-, 6- or 7-quart **CROCK-POT**® slow cooker, cut any piece of meat larger than 2½ pounds in half so it cooks completely.*

1. Place onion in **CROCK-POT**® slow cooker. Combine garlic, rosemary and pepper in small bowl.

2. Cut slices about three fourths of the way through turkey at 2-inch intervals. Rub garlic mixture between slices. Place turkey, cut side up, in **CROCK-POT**® slow cooker. Pour orange juice over turkey. Cover; cook on LOW 7 to 8 hours.

3. Slice turkey. Serve over rice, if desired, with orange sauce.

Makes 4 to 6 servings

Chipotle Turkey Sloppy Joe Sliders

1 pound turkey Italian sausage, casings removed

1 package (14 ounces) frozen green and red bell pepper strips with onions

1 can (6 ounces) tomato paste

1 tablespoon quick-cooking tapioca

1 tablespoon minced canned chipotle pepper in adobo sauce, plus 1 tablespoon sauce

2 teaspoons ground cumin

½ teaspoon dried thyme

12 corn muffins or small dinner rolls, split and toasted

1. Brown sausage in large skillet over medium-high heat 6 to 8 minutes, stirring to break up meat. Drain fat. Remove to **CROCK-POT®** slow cooker.

2. Stir in pepper strips with onions, tomato paste, tapioca, chipotle pepper and sauce, cumin and thyme. Cover; cook on LOW 8 to 10 hours. Serve on corn muffins.

Makes 12 sliders

Italian Stew

- **1 can (about 14 ounces) chicken broth**
- **1 can (about 14 ounces) Italian stewed tomatoes with peppers and onions, undrained**
- **1 package (9 ounces) fully cooked spicy chicken sausage, sliced**
- **2 small zucchini, sliced**
- **2 carrots, thinly sliced**
- **1 can (about 15 ounces) Great Northern, cannellini or navy beans, rinsed and drained**
- **2 tablespoons chopped fresh basil (optional)**

1. Combine broth, tomatoes, sausage, zucchini and carrots in **CROCK-POT®** slow cooker. Cover; cook on LOW 6 to 7 hours or on HIGH 3 to 4 hours.

2. Stir in beans. Cover; cook on HIGH 10 to 15 minutes or until beans are heated through. Ladle into shallow bowls. Garnish with basil.

Makes 6 servings

Nutrition Information

Serving Size: about 1 cup

Calories 293
Total Fat 7g
Saturated Fat 2g
Protein 24g
Carbohydrate 38g
Cholesterol 46mg
Fiber 8g
Sodium 134mg

Dietary Exchanges:
2½ Starch, 2 Meat

Nutrition Information

Serving Size: 1 chicken thigh with about ¾ cup olive mixture and ¼ cup rice

Calories 290
Total Fat 9g
Saturated Fat 2g
Protein 31g
Carbohydrate 18g
Cholesterol 140mg
Fiber 2g
Sodium................. 510mg

Dietary Exchanges:
1 Starch, 1 Vegetable,
4 Meat, 1 Fat

Provençal Lemon and Olive Chicken

 2 **cups chopped onion**
 6 **boneless, skinless chicken thighs (about 2 pounds)**
 1 **medium lemon, thinly sliced and seeds removed**
 ½ **cup pitted green olives**
 1 **tablespoon white vinegar or olive brine from jar**
 2 **teaspoons herbes de Provence**
 1 **whole bay leaf**
 ⅛ **teaspoon black pepper**
 1 **cup fat-free reduced-sodium chicken broth**
 ½ **cup minced fresh Italian parsley**
 1½ **cups hot cooked rice**

1. Place onion in **CROCK-POT®** slow cooker. Arrange chicken thighs over onion. Place lemon slice on each thigh. Add olives, vinegar, herbes de Provence, bay leaf and pepper; slowly pour in broth.

2. Cover; cook on LOW 5 to 6 hours or on HIGH 3 to 3½ hours. Remove and discard bay leaf. Stir in parsley. Serve over rice.

Makes 6 servings

Chicken and Sweet Potato Stew

Nutrition Information

Serving Size: about 1 cup

Calories 200
Total Fat 2g
Saturated Fat 0g
Protein 20g
Carbohydrate 26g
Cholesterol 50mg
Fiber 5g
Sodium 600mg

Dietary Exchanges:
1 Starch, 2 Vegetable, 2 Meat

Tip

Recipe can be doubled for a 5-, 6- or 7-quart **CROCK-POT**® slow cooker.

- **4** boneless, skinless chicken breasts, cut into 1-inch pieces
- **2** medium sweet potatoes, peeled and cubed
- **2** medium Yukon Gold potatoes, peeled and cubed
- **2** medium carrots, cut into ½-inch slices
- **1** can (28 ounces) reduced-sodium whole stewed tomatoes
- **1** cup fat-free reduced-sodium chicken broth
- **1** teaspoon salt
- **1** teaspoon paprika
- **1** teaspoon celery seed
- **½** teaspoon black pepper
- **⅛** teaspoon ground cinnamon
- **⅛** teaspoon ground nutmeg
- **¼** cup fresh basil, chopped

Combine chicken, potatoes, carrots, tomatoes, broth, salt, paprika, celery seeds, pepper, cinnamon and nutmeg in **CROCK-POT**® slow cooker; stir to blend. Cover; cook on LOW 6 to 8 hours or on HIGH 3 to 4 hours. Sprinkle with basil just before serving.

Makes 6 servings

Mu Shu Turkey

Nutrition Information

Serving Size: 1 filled tortilla

Calories 248
Total Fat 4g
Saturated Fat 1g
Protein 17g
Carbohydrate 36g
Cholesterol 30mg
Fiber 3g
Sodium 282mg

Dietary Exchanges:
½ Starch, 1 Vegetable, 1 Fruit, 2 Meat

- **1 can (16 ounces) plums, drained and pitted**
- **½ cup orange juice**
- **¼ cup finely chopped onion**
- **1 tablespoon minced fresh ginger**
- **¼ teaspoon ground cinnamon**
- **1 pound boneless, skinless turkey breast, cut into thin strips**
- **6 (7-inch) flour tortillas, warmed**
- **3 cups coleslaw mix**
- **Orange wedges (optional)**

1. Place plums in blender or food processor; blend until almost smooth. Combine plums, orange juice, onion, ginger and cinnamon in **CROCK-POT®** slow cooker; mix well. Place turkey over plum mixture. Cover; cook on LOW 3 to 4 hours.

2. Divide turkey evenly among tortillas. Spoon 2 tablespoons plum sauce over turkey; top with ½ cup coleslaw mix. Fold up bottom edges of tortillas over filling, fold in sides and roll up to enclose filling. Serve with remaining plum sauce and oranges, if desired.

Makes 6 servings

Serving Size: about
1 cup sausage mixture
with ½ cup pasta

Calories 310
Total Fat 12g
Saturated Fat 4g
Protein 19g
Carbohydrate 27g
Cholesterol 50mg
Fiber 6g
Sodium 780mg

Dietary Exchanges:
1 Starch, 2 Vegetable,
2 Meat, 2 Fat

Chicken Sausage with Peppers & Basil

1	tablespoon olive oil
½	medium yellow onion, minced (about ½ cup)
1	clove garlic, minced
1	pound sweet or hot Italian chicken sausage
1	can (28 ounces) whole tomatoes, drained and seeded
½	medium red bell pepper, cut into ½-inch slices
½	medium yellow bell pepper, cut into ½-inch slices
½	medium orange bell pepper, cut into ½-inch slices
¾	cup chopped fresh basil
3	cups hot cooked rotini pasta

1. Heat oil in large skillet over medium heat. Add onion and garlic; cook until translucent.

2. Remove sausage from casings; cut into 1-inch pieces. Add to skillet; cook 3 to 4 minutes or until just beginning to brown. Remove to **CROCK-POT®** slow cooker with slotted spoon.

3. Add tomatoes, bell peppers and basil to **CROCK-POT®** slow cooker; stir to blend. Cover; cook on HIGH 2½ to 3 hours or until bell peppers have softened. Serve over pasta.

Makes 6 servings

Citrus Mangoretto Chicken

Nutrition Information

Serving Size: 1 chicken breast with about ¼ cup mango mixture

Calories 210
Total Fat........................4g
Saturated Fat................1g
Protein 25g
Carbohydrate 16g
Cholesterol 75mg
Fiber 1g
Sodium................. 370mg

Dietary Exchanges:
½ Fruit, 3 Meat

Variation

Refrigerate any leftover chicken and sauce. Serve over salad greens.

- 4 **boneless, skinless chicken breasts (about 1 pound)**
- 1 **large ripe mango, peeled and diced**
- 3 **tablespoons lime juice**
- 1 **tablespoon grated lime peel**
- ¼ **cup Amaretto liqueur**
- 1 **tablespoon chopped fresh rosemary *or* 1 teaspoon dried rosemary**
- 1 **cup fat-free chicken broth**
- 1 **tablespoon water**
- 2 **teaspoons cornstarch**

1. Place 2 chicken breasts side by side on bottom of **CROCK-POT**® slow cooker.

2. Combine mango, lime juice, lime peel, Amaretto and rosemary in medium bowl; stir to blend. Spread half of mango mixture over chicken in **CROCK-POT**® slow cooker. Lay remaining 2 chicken breasts on top crosswise, and spread with remaining mango mixture. Carefully pour broth around edges of chicken. Cover; cook on LOW 3 to 4 hours.

3. Turn **CROCK-POT**® slow cooker to HIGH. Stir water into cornstarch in small bowl until smooth; whisk into cooking liquid. Cover; cook on HIGH 15 minutes or until sauce is thickened. Serve mango and sauce over chicken.

Makes 4 servings

Creamy Chicken Sausage Rice Pilaf

- **1 box (4 ounces) wild rice**
- **½ cup uncooked brown basmati rice**
- **1 package (12 ounces) fully cooked chicken apple sausage, cut into ½-inch slices**
- **3 medium carrots, chopped**
- **1 medium onion, chopped**
- **½ cup sweetened dried cranberries**
- **1 teaspoon dried oregano**
- **¾ teaspoon salt**
- **¼ teaspoon black pepper**
- **3 cups water**
- **½ cup whipping cream**

Combine wild rice, basmati rice, chicken sausage, carrots, onion, cranberries, oregano, salt and pepper in **CROCK-POT**® slow cooker. Cover; cook on LOW 7 to 8 hours or until rice is tender. Turn off heat. Stir in cream and let stand 10 minutes before serving.

Makes 8 servings

VEGETARIAN MAIN DISHES

Curried Lentils with Fruit

- **5 cups water**
- **1½ cups dried brown lentils, rinsed and sorted**
- **1 Granny Smith apple, chopped, plus additional for garnish**
- **¼ cup golden raisins**
- **¼ cup lemon nonfat yogurt**
- **1 teaspoon salt**
- **1 teaspoon curry powder**

1. Combine water, lentils, 1 apple and raisins in **CROCK-POT®** slow cooker. Cover; cook on LOW 8 to 9 hours or until lentils are tender. (Lentils should absorb most or all of the water. Slightly tilt **CROCK-POT®** slow cooker to check.)

2. Remove lentil mixture to large bowl; stir in yogurt, salt and curry powder until blended. Garnish with additional apple.

Makes 6 servings

Nutrition Information

Serving Size: ½ cup

Calories 160
Total Fat 1g
Saturated Fat 1g
Protein 10g
Carbohydrate 31g
Cholesterol 1mg
Fiber 6g
Sodium................ 364mg

Dietary Exchanges:
2 Starch, ½ Fruit

Vegetarian Paella

  2 **teaspoons canola oil**
  1 **cup chopped onion**
  2 **cloves garlic, minced**
  1 **cup uncooked brown rice**
2¼ **cups vegetable broth**
  1 **can (about 14 ounces) no-salt-added stewed tomatoes**
  1 **small zucchini, halved lengthwise and sliced to ½-inch thickness (about 1¼ cups)**
  1 **cup coarsely chopped carrots**
  1 **cup chopped red bell pepper**
  1 **teaspoon Italian seasoning**
  ½ **teaspoon ground turmeric**
  ⅛ **teaspoon ground red pepper**
  1 **can (about 14 ounces) quartered artichoke hearts, drained**
  ½ **cup frozen baby peas**

1. Heat oil in large skillet over medium-high heat. Add onion; cook and stir 6 to 7 minutes or until tender. Stir in garlic.

2. Combine onion mixture and rice in **CROCK-POT**® slow cooker. Add broth, tomatoes, zucchini, carrots, bell pepper, Italian seasoning, turmeric and ground red pepper; mix well. Cover; cook on LOW 4 hours or on HIGH 2 hours or until liquid is absorbed.

3. Stir in artichokes and peas. Cover; cook on LOW 5 to 10 minutes or until vegetables are tender.

Makes 6 servings

Nutrition Information

Serving Size: ½ cup

Calories 96
Total Fat......................2g
Saturated Fat...............1g
Protein 7g
Carbohydrate 17g
Cholesterol 4mg
Fiber 7g
Sodium...................98mg

Dietary Exchanges:
3 Vegetable, ½ Fat

Ratatouille
with Parmesan Cheese

Nonstick cooking spray
1 **cup diced eggplant**
2 **medium tomatoes, chopped**
1 **small zucchini, diced**
1 **cup sliced mushrooms**
½ **cup tomato purée**
1 **large shallot** *or* ½ **small onion, chopped**
1 **clove garlic, minced**
¾ **teaspoon dried oregano**
⅛ **teaspoon dried rosemary**
⅛ **teaspoon black pepper**
2 **tablespoons shredded fresh basil**
2 **teaspoons lemon juice**
¼ **teaspoon salt**
Grated Parmesan cheese (optional)

1. Spray large skillet with cooking spray; heat over medium-high heat. Add eggplant; cook and stir 5 minutes or until lightly browned. Remove eggplant to **CROCK-POT®** slow cooker.

2. Add tomatoes, zucchini, mushrooms, tomato purée, shallot, garlic, oregano, rosemary and pepper; stir to blend. Cover; cook on LOW 6 hours or on HIGH 3 hours.

3. Stir in basil, lemon juice and salt. Turn off heat; let stand 5 minutes. Top each serving evenly with Parmesan cheese, if desired.

Makes 4 servings

Polenta Lasagna

　4　**cups boiling water**
1½　**cups whole grain yellow cornmeal**
　4　**teaspoons finely chopped fresh marjoram**
　1　**teaspoon olive oil**
　1　**pound mushrooms, sliced**
　1　**cup chopped leeks**
　1　**clove garlic, minced**
　½　**cup (2 ounces) shredded mozzarella cheese**
　2　**tablespoons chopped fresh basil**
　1　**tablespoon chopped fresh oregano**
　⅛　**teaspoon black pepper**
　2　**medium red bell peppers, chopped**
　¼　**cup water**
　¼　**cup freshly grated Parmesan cheese, divided**

1. Coat inside of **CROCK-POT®** slow cooker with nonstick cooking spray. Combine 4 cups boiling water and cornmeal in **CROCK-POT®** slow cooker; mix well. Stir in marjoram. Cover; cook on LOW 3 to 4 hours or on HIGH 1 to 2 hours, stirring occasionally. Cover; chill 1 hour or until firm.

2. Heat oil in medium nonstick skillet over medium heat. Add mushrooms, leeks and garlic; cook and stir 5 minutes or until leeks are crisp-tender. Stir in mozzarella cheese, basil, oregano and black pepper. Place bell peppers and ¼ cup water in food processor or blender; process until smooth.

3. Cut cold polenta in half and place one half on bottom of **CROCK-POT®** slow cooker. Top with half of bell pepper mixture, half of vegetable mixture and 2 tablespoons Parmesan cheese. Place remaining polenta over Parmesan cheese; layer with remaining bell pepper and vegetable mixtures and Parmesan cheese. Cover; cook on LOW 3 hours or until cheese is melted and polenta is golden brown. Cut into six squares.

Makes 6 servings

Mushroom and Vegetable Ragoût over Polenta

- **3 tablespoons extra virgin olive oil**
- **8 ounces sliced mushrooms**
- **8 ounces shiitake mushrooms, stemmed and thinly sliced**
- **½ cup Madeira wine**
- **4 cloves garlic, minced**
- **1 medium onion, chopped**
- **1 can (about 15 ounces) low-sodium chickpeas, rinsed and drained**
- **1 can (about 28 ounces) crushed tomatoes**
- **1 can (about 6 ounces) tomato paste**
- **1 sprig fresh rosemary, plus additional for garnish**
- **2 cups water**
- **2 cups reduced-fat (2%) milk**
- **¼ teaspoon salt**
- **2 cups instant polenta**
- **½ cup grated Parmesan cheese**

1. Heat oil in large skillet over medium-high heat. Add mushrooms; cook and stir 8 to 10 minutes or until mushrooms are browned. Add wine; cook 1 minute or until liquid is reduced by half. Remove to **CROCK-POT**® slow cooker.

2. Stir in garlic, onion, chickpeas, crushed tomatoes, tomato paste and 1 sprig rosemary. Cover; cook on LOW 6 hours. Remove and discard rosemary.

3. Combine water, milk and salt in large saucepan over medium-high heat. Bring to a boil. Whisk in polenta in slow, steady stream. Cook and whisk 4 to 5 minutes or until thick and creamy. Remove polenta from heat. Stir in cheese; top with ragoût. Garnish with additional rosemary.

Makes 8 servings

Vegetable Pasta Sauce

Nutrition Information

Serving Size: 2 cups
sauce with ½ cup pasta

Calories 190
Total Fat.......................1g
Saturated Fat 0g
Protein 8g
Carbohydrate 38g
Cholesterol 0mg
Fiber 7g
Sodium................ 390mg

Dietary Exchanges:
1 Starch, 4 Vegetable

   2 **cans (about 14 ounces *each*) unsalted diced tomatoes**
   1 **can (about 14 ounces) whole tomatoes, undrained**
1½ **cups sliced mushrooms**
   1 **medium red bell pepper, chopped**
   1 **medium green bell pepper, chopped**
   1 **small yellow squash, cut into ¼-inch slices**
   1 **small zucchini, cut into ¼-inch slices**
   1 **can (6 ounces) tomato paste**
   4 **green onions, sliced**
   3 **cloves garlic, minced**
   2 **tablespoons Italian seasoning**
   1 **tablespoon chopped fresh Italian parsley**
   1 **teaspoon red pepper flakes (optional)**
   1 **teaspoon black pepper**
   3 **cups hot cooked penne pasta**
       Parmesan cheese and fresh basil leaves (optional)

Combine tomatoes, mushrooms, bell peppers, squash, zucchini, tomato paste, green onions, garlic, Italian seasoning, parsley, red pepper flakes, if desired, and black pepper in **CROCK-POT**® slow cooker; stir to blend. Cover; cook on LOW 6 to 8 hours. Serve over pasta. Top with cheese and basil, if desired.

Makes 6 servings

Lentil and Spinach Stew

Nutrition Information

Serving Size: 1 cup stew with ¼ cup pasta

Calories 290
Total Fat........................4g
Saturated Fat 1g
Protein 14g
Carbohydrate 51g
Cholesterol 0mg
Fiber 14g
Sodium.................500mg

Dietary Exchanges:
2½ Starch, 2 Vegetable, ½ Fat

1　**tablespoon olive oil**
3　**medium stalks celery, cut into ½-inch pieces**
3　**medium carrots, cut into ½-inch pieces**
1　**medium onion, chopped**
3　**cloves garlic, minced**
1　**can (about 14 ounces) diced tomatoes**
1　**cup dried brown lentils, rinsed and sorted***
2　**teaspoons ground cumin**
½　**teaspoon dried basil**
4　**cups reduced-sodium vegetable broth**
½　**teaspoon salt**
¼　**teaspoon black pepper**
5　**cups baby spinach**
⅓　**pound uncooked ditalini pasta**

Packages of dried lentils may contain dirt and tiny stones. So, thoroughly rinse lentils, then sort through them and discard any unusual-looking pieces.

1. Heat oil in large skillet over medium-high heat. Add celery, carrots, onion and garlic; cook and stir 3 to 4 minutes or until vegetables begin to soften.

2. Coat inside of **CROCK-POT**® slow cooker with nonstick cooking spray. Remove vegetable mixture to **CROCK-POT**® slow cooker. Stir in tomatoes, lentils, cumin, basil, broth, salt and pepper. Cover; cook on LOW 8 to 9 hours or until lentils are tender but still hold their shape.

3. Stir in spinach just before serving. Prepare pasta according to package directions. Serve stew over pasta.

Makes 6 servings

Spring Vegetable Ragoût

1 **tablespoon olive oil**

2 **leeks, thinly sliced**

3 **cloves garlic, minced**

3 **cups small cherry tomatoes, halved**

1 **package (10 ounces) frozen corn**

1 **cup vegetable broth**

½ **pound yellow squash, halved lengthwise and cut into ½-inch pieces (about 1¼ cups)**

1 **small bag (6 ounces) frozen edamame (soybeans), shelled**

1 **small bag (4 ounces) shredded carrots**

1 **teaspoon dried tarragon**

1 **teaspoon dried basil**

1 **teaspoon dried oregano**

Salt and black pepper (optional)

Minced fresh Italian parsley (optional)

1. Heat oil in large skillet over medium heat. Add leeks and garlic; cook and stir just until fragrant.

2. Stir leeks and garlic mixture, tomatoes, corn, broth, squash, edamame, carrots, tarragon, basil and oregano into **CROCK-POT**® slow cooker. Cover; cook on LOW 6 to 8 hours or on HIGH 3 to 4 hours or until vegetables are tender. Season to taste with salt and pepper, if desired. Garnish with parsley.

Makes 6 servings

Mexican Hot Pot

1 tablespoon canola oil

1 medium onion, chopped

3 cloves garlic, minced

2 teaspoons red pepper flakes

2 teaspoons dried oregano

1 teaspoon ground cumin

1 can (28 ounces) whole tomatoes, drained and chopped

2 cups corn

1 can (about 15 ounces) chickpeas, rinsed and drained

1 can (about 15 ounces) pinto beans, rinsed and drained

1 cup water

6 cups shredded iceberg lettuce

1. Heat oil in large skillet over medium-high heat. Add onion and garlic; cook and stir 5 minutes. Add red pepper flakes, oregano and cumin; mix well.

2. Remove onion and garlic mixture to **CROCK-POT®** slow cooker. Stir in tomatoes, corn, chickpeas, beans and water. Cover; cook on LOW 7 to 8 hours or on HIGH 2 to 3 hours. Top each serving with 1 cup shredded lettuce.

Makes 6 servings

Red Beans and Rice

2 **cans (about 15 ounces *each*) red beans, undrained**
1 **can (about 14 ounces) diced tomatoes**
½ **cup chopped celery**
½ **cup chopped green bell pepper**
½ **cup chopped green onions**
2 **cloves garlic, minced**
1 **to 2 teaspoons hot pepper sauce**
1 **teaspoon Worcestershire sauce**
1 **whole bay leaf**
3 **cups hot cooked rice**

1. Combine beans, tomatoes, celery, bell pepper, green onions, garlic, hot pepper sauce, Worcestershire sauce and bay leaf in **CROCK-POT**® slow cooker; stir to blend. Cover; cook on LOW 4 to 6 hours or on HIGH 2 to 3 hours.

2. Mash bean mixture slightly in **CROCK-POT**® slow cooker until mixture thickens. Cover; cook on HIGH ½ to 1 hour. Remove and discard bay leaf. Serve bean mixture over rice.

Makes 6 servings

Southwestern Beans and Vegetables

Nutrition Information

Serving Size: ½ cup

Calories 84
Total Fat........................1g
Saturated Fat 0g
Protein 5g
Carbohydrate 20g
Cholesterol 0mg
Fiber 6g
Sodium.................. 421mg

Dietary Exchanges:
1 Starch

1 **can (about 15 ounces) black beans, rinsed and drained**

½ **cup frozen corn**

½ **cup reduced-sodium vegetable broth**

1 **large shallot *or* ½ small onion, finely chopped**

1 **small jalapeño pepper, cored, seeded and minced***

1 **clove garlic, minced**

¼ **teaspoon ground cumin**

⅛ **teaspoon black pepper**

1 **tablespoon finely chopped fresh cilantro**

1 **tablespoon lime juice**

¼ **teaspoon salt (optional)**

Jalapeño peppers can sting and irritate the skin, so wear rubber gloves when handling peppers and do not touch your eyes.

1. Stir beans, corn, broth, shallot, jalapeño pepper, garlic, cumin and black pepper into **CROCK-POT®** slow cooker. Cover; cook on LOW 5 to 6 hours.

2. Stir cilantro, lime juice and salt, if desired, into **CROCK-POT®** slow cooker. Turn off heat; let stand 5 minutes before serving.

Makes 4 servings

Artichoke and Tomato Paella

4 cups vegetable broth

2 cups uncooked converted rice

5 ounces (½ of 10-ounce package) frozen chopped spinach, thawed and drained

1 medium green bell pepper, chopped

1 medium tomato, sliced into wedges

1 medium yellow onion, chopped

1 medium carrot, diced

3 cloves garlic, minced

1 tablespoon minced Italian parsley

½ teaspoon black pepper

1 can (13¾ ounces) artichoke hearts, quartered, rinsed and well drained

½ cup frozen peas

Combine broth, rice, spinach, bell pepper, tomato, onion, carrot, garlic, parsley and black pepper in **CROCK-POT®** slow cooker; stir to blend. Cover; cook on LOW 4 hours or on HIGH 2 hours. Stir in artichoke hearts and peas. Cover; cook on HIGH 15 minutes.

Makes 8 servings

Manchego Eggplant

1 cup all-purpose flour

4 large eggplants, peeled and sliced horizontally into ¾-inch-thick slices

2 tablespoons olive oil

1 jar (24 to 26 ounces) roasted garlic-flavor pasta sauce

2 tablespoons Italian seasoning

1 cup grated manchego cheese

1 jar (24 to 26 ounces) roasted eggplant-flavor marinara sauce

Sprigs fresh basil (optional)

1. Place flour in medium shallow bowl. Add eggplant; toss to coat. Heat oil in large skillet over medium-high heat. Lightly brown eggplant in batches 3 to 4 minutes on each side.

2. Pour thin layer of garlic pasta sauce into bottom of **CROCK-POT®** slow cooker. Top with half of eggplant slices, Italian seasoning, cheese and marinara sauce. Repeat layers with remaining half of eggplant slices, Italian seasoning, cheese and marinara sauce. Cover; cook on HIGH 2 hours. Garnish with basil.

Makes 12 servings

Slow Cooker Veggie Stew

Nutrition Information

Serving Size: 1 cup

Calories 90
Total Fat 4g
Saturated Fat 1g
Protein 2g
Carbohydrate 10g
Cholesterol 0mg
Fiber 3g
Sodium 400mg

Dietary Exchanges:
2 Vegetable, 1 Fat

 1 **tablespoon vegetable oil**
 ¾ **cup carrot slices**
 ½ **cup diced onion**
 2 **cloves garlic, chopped**
 2 **cans (about 14 ounces *each*) fat-free reduced-sodium vegetable broth**
1½ **cups chopped green cabbage**
 ½ **cup cut green beans**
 ½ **cup diced zucchini**
 1 **tablespoon tomato paste**
 ½ **teaspoon dried basil**
 ½ **teaspoon dried oregano**
 ¼ **teaspoon salt**

1. Heat oil in medium skillet over medium-high heat. Add carrot, onion and garlic; cook and stir 8 minutes or until tender.

2. Remove carrot mixture to **CROCK-POT®** slow cooker. Add broth, cabbage, beans, zucchini, tomato paste, basil, oregano and salt; stir to combine. Cover; cook on LOW 8 to 10 hours or on HIGH 4 to 5 hours.

Makes 4 servings

Black Bean Stuffed Peppers

Nonstick cooking spray

1   medium onion, finely chopped

¼   teaspoon ground red pepper

¼   teaspoon dried oregano

¼   teaspoon ground cumin

¼   teaspoon chili powder

1   can (about 15 ounces) black beans, rinsed and drained

6   large green bell peppers, tops removed

1   cup (4 ounces) shredded Monterey Jack cheese

1   cup tomato salsa

½   cup sour cream

1. Spray medium skillet with cooking spray; heat over medium heat. Add onion; cook and stir 3 to 5 minutes or until golden. Add ground red pepper, oregano, cumin and chili powder; cook and stir 1 minute.

2. Mash half of beans with onion mixture in medium bowl; stir in remaining half of beans. Spoon black bean mixture evenly into bell peppers; sprinkle with cheese. Pour salsa over cheese. Place bell peppers in **CROCK-POT®** slow cooker.

3. Cover; cook on LOW 6 to 8 hours or on HIGH 3 to 4 hours. Serve with sour cream.

Makes 6 servings

Nutrition Information

Serving Size: 1 pepper

Calories 180
Total Fat.......................5g
Saturated Fat..............3g
Protein 11g
Carbohydrate 25g
Cholesterol 10mg
Fiber 6g
Sodium................ 550mg

Dietary Exchanges:
1 Starch, 2 Vegetable,
2 Meat

Tip

You may increase any of the recipe ingredients to taste except the tomato salsa, and use a 5-, 6- or 7-quart **CROCK-POT®** slow cooker. However, the peppers should fit comfortably in a single layer in your stoneware.

Asian Golden Barley with Cashews

Nutrition Information

Serving Size: 2 cups

Calories 300
Total Fat 12g
Saturated Fat 2g
Protein 8g
Carbohydrate 43g
Cholesterol 0mg
Fiber 10g
Sodium 750mg

Dietary Exchanges:
2 Starch, 1 Vegetable,
2 Fat

2 tablespoons olive oil

1 cup uncooked hulled barley, sorted

3 cups vegetable broth

1 cup chopped celery

1 medium green bell pepper, chopped

1 medium yellow onion, peeled and minced

1 clove garlic, minced

¼ teaspoon black pepper

1 ounce finely chopped cashew nuts

1. Heat large skillet over medium heat. Add oil and barley; cook and stir 10 minutes or until barley is slightly browned. Remove to **CROCK-POT®** slow cooker.

2. Add broth, celery, bell pepper, onion, garlic and black pepper; stir to blend. Cover; cook on LOW 4 to 5 hours or on HIGH 2 to 3 hours or until barley is tender and liquid is absorbed.

3. Top each serving evenly with cashews.

Makes 4 servings

Lentil Stew over Couscous

Nutrition Information

Serving Size: ½ of lentil stew with about ⅓ cup cooked couscous

Calories 203
Total Fat 2g
Saturated Fat 1g
Protein 11g
Carbohydrate 37g
Cholesterol 0mg
Fiber 4g
Sodium................. 128mg

Dietary Exchanges:
2 Starch, 1 Vegetable,
½ Meat

Variation

Instead of couscous,
serve stew over
cooked quinoa.

3 cups dried lentils (1 pound), sorted and rinsed
3 cups water
1 can (about 14 ounces) fat-free reduced-sodium vegetable broth
1 can (about 14 ounces) diced tomatoes
1 large onion, chopped
1 green bell pepper, chopped
4 stalks celery, chopped
1 medium carrot, halved lengthwise and sliced
2 cloves garlic, chopped
1 teaspoon dried marjoram
¼ teaspoon black pepper
1 tablespoon olive oil
1 tablespoon cider vinegar
4½ to 5 cups hot cooked couscous

1. Combine lentils, water, broth, tomatoes, onion, bell pepper, celery, carrot, garlic, marjoram and black pepper in **CROCK-POT**® slow cooker; stir to blend. Cover; cook on LOW 8 to 9 hours or until vegetables are tender.

2. Stir in oil and vinegar. Serve over couscous.

Makes 12 servings

Three-Bean Chipotle Chili

2 tablespoons olive oil
1 large onion, chopped
1 medium green bell pepper, chopped
2 cloves garlic, minced
2 cans (about 15 ounces *each*) pinto beans, rinsed and drained
1 can (about 15 ounces) small white beans, rinsed and drained
1 can (about 15 ounces) chickpeas, rinsed and drained
1 cup water
1 cup frozen or canned corn
1 can (6 ounces) tomato paste
1 or 2 canned chipotle peppers in adobo sauce, finely chopped
   Optional toppings: sour cream, shredded Cheddar cheese and/or chopped fresh chives
   Tortilla chips (optional)

1. Heat oil in large skillet over medium heat. Add onion, bell pepper and garlic; cook and stir 5 minutes or until onion is softened. Remove to **CROCK-POT**® slow cooker.

2. Stir in beans, chickpeas, water, corn, tomato paste and chipotle pepper. Cover; cook on LOW 3½ to 4 hours. Top as desired. Serve with chips, if desired.

Makes 8 servings

Italian Eggplant with Millet and Pepper Stuffing

¼ cup uncooked millet

2 small eggplants (about ¾ pound total), unpeeled

¼ cup chopped red bell pepper, divided

¼ cup chopped green bell pepper, divided

1 teaspoon olive oil

1 clove garlic, minced

1½ cups fat-free reduced-sodium vegetable broth

½ teaspoon ground cumin

½ teaspoon dried oregano

⅛ teaspoon red pepper flakes

Sprigs fresh basil (optional)

1. Heat large skillet over medium heat. Add millet; cook and stir 5 minutes. Remove to small bowl; set aside. Cut eggplants lengthwise into halves. Scoop out flesh, leaving about ¼-inch-thick shell. Reserve shells; chop eggplant flesh. Combine 1 tablespoon red bell pepper and 1 tablespoon green bell pepper in small bowl; set aside.

2. Heat oil in same skillet over medium heat. Add chopped eggplant, remaining red and green bell peppers and garlic; cook and stir 8 minutes or until eggplant is tender.

3. Combine eggplant mixture, broth, cumin, oregano and red pepper flakes in **CROCK-POT**® slow cooker. Cover; cook on LOW 4½ hours or until all liquid is absorbed.

4. Turn **CROCK-POT**® slow cooker to HIGH. Fill eggplant shells with eggplant-millet mixture. Sprinkle with reserved bell peppers. Place filled shells in **CROCK-POT**® slow cooker. Cover; cook on HIGH 1½ to 2 hours. Garnish with basil.

Makes 4 servings

Nutrition Information

Serving Size: 1¼ cups

Calories 193
Total Fat..................... 2g
Saturated Fat 1g
Protein 6g
Carbohydrate 40g
Cholesterol 0mg
Fiber 6g
Sodium.................. 194mg

Dietary Exchanges:
2½ Starch, ½ Vegetable

Quinoa and Vegetable Medley

2 medium sweet potatoes, cut into ½-inch-thick slices
1 medium eggplant, cut into ½-inch cubes
1 large green bell pepper, sliced
1 medium tomato, cut into wedges
1 small onion, cut into wedges
½ teaspoon salt
¼ teaspoon ground red pepper
¼ teaspoon black pepper
1 cup uncooked quinoa
2 cups fat-free reduced-sodium vegetable broth
2 cloves garlic, minced
½ teaspoon dried thyme
¼ teaspoon dried marjoram

1. Coat inside of **CROCK-POT**® slow cooker with nonstick cooking spray. Combine potatoes, eggplant, bell pepper, tomato, onion, salt, ground red pepper and black pepper in **CROCK-POT**® slow cooker; toss to coat.

2. Place quinoa in strainer; rinse well. Add quinoa to vegetable mixture in **CROCK-POT**® slow cooker. Stir in broth, garlic, thyme and marjoram. Cover; cook on LOW 5 hours or on HIGH 2½ hours or until quinoa is tender and broth is absorbed.

Makes 6 servings

Slow-Cooked Succotash

  2 teaspoons canola oil
  1 cup diced onion
  1 cup diced green bell pepper
  1 cup diced celery
  1 teaspoon paprika
  1½ cups frozen corn
  1½ cups frozen lima beans
  1 cup canned reduced-sodium diced tomatoes
  2 teaspoons dried parsley flakes *or* 1 tablespoon minced fresh Italian parsley
  ½ teaspoon salt
  ½ teaspoon black pepper

1. Heat oil in large skillet over medium heat. Add onion, bell pepper and celery; cook and stir 5 minutes or until onion is translucent and bell pepper and celery are crisp-tender. Stir in paprika.

2. Stir onion mixture, corn, beans, tomatoes, parsley flakes, salt and black pepper into **CROCK-POT**® slow cooker. Cover; cook on LOW 6 to 8 hours or on HIGH 3 to 4 hours.

Makes 8 servings

Nutrition Information

Serving Size: 1½ cups

Calories 99
Total Fat........................2g
Saturated Fat 1g
Protein 4g
Carbohydrate 19g
Cholesterol 0mg
Fiber 4g
Sodium................. 187mg

Dietary Exchanges:
1 Starch, ½ Fat

Nutrition Information

Serving Size: 1½ cups

Calories 146
Total Fat 2g
Saturated Fat 1g
Protein 8g
Carbohydrate 24g
Cholesterol 0mg
Fiber 6g
Sodium 209mg

Dietary Exchanges:
1½ Starch, ½ Meat, ½ Fat

Confetti Black Beans

1	**cup dried black beans**
3	**cups water**
1½	**teaspoons olive oil**
1	**medium onion, chopped**
¼	**cup chopped red bell pepper**
¼	**cup chopped yellow bell pepper**
1	**jalapeño pepper, finely chopped***
1	**large tomato, seeded and chopped**
½	**teaspoon salt**
⅛	**teaspoon black pepper**
2	**cloves garlic, minced**
1	**can (about 14 ounces) reduced-sodium chicken broth**
1	**whole bay leaf**
	Hot pepper sauce (optional)

Jalapeño peppers can sting and irritate the skin, so wear rubber gloves when handling peppers and do not touch your eyes.

1. Rinse and sort beans; cover with water. Soak 8 hours or overnight.** Drain.

2. Heat oil in large skillet over medium heat. Add onion, bell peppers and jalapeño pepper; cook and stir 5 minutes or until onion is tender. Add tomato, salt and black pepper; cook 5 minutes. Stir in garlic.

3. Place beans, broth and bay leaf in **CROCK-POT**® slow cooker. Add onion mixture. Cover; cook on LOW 7 to 8 hours or on HIGH 4½ to 5 hours or until beans are tender. Remove and discard bay leaf. Serve with hot pepper sauce, if desired.

**To quick soak beans, place beans in large saucepan; cover with water. Bring to a boil over high heat. Boil 2 minutes. Remove from heat; let soak, covered, 1 hour.

Makes 6 servings

Nutrition Information

Serving Size: about ¾ cup

Calories 230
Total Fat 6g
Saturated Fat 1g
Protein 5g
Carbohydrate 41g
Cholesterol 0mg
Fiber 4g
Sodium 770mg

Dietary Exchanges:
1½ Starch, 1½ Vegetable, 1 Fat

Tip

Jollof Rice (also spelled "jolof") is an important dish in many West African cultures.

Vegetable Jollof Rice

1 **medium eggplant (about 1¼ pounds), trimmed and cut into 1-inch cubes**
1½ **teaspoons salt, divided**
3 **tablespoons vegetable oil, divided**
1 **medium onion, chopped**
1 **medium green bell pepper, chopped**
3 **medium carrots, cut into ½-inch-thick rounds**
2 **cloves garlic, minced**
1½ **cups uncooked converted rice**
1 **tablespoon plus ½ teaspoon chili powder**
1 **can (about 28 ounces) diced tomatoes, undrained**
1 **can (about 14 ounces) reduced-sodium vegetable broth**

1. Place eggplant cubes in colander. Toss with 1 teaspoon salt. Let stand 1 hour to drain. Rinse under cold running water; drain and pat dry with paper towels.

2. Heat 2 tablespoons oil in large skillet over medium-high heat. Working in batches, add eggplant to skillet; cook and stir until brown on all sides. Remove to plate; set aside.

3. Wipe out skillet with paper towels. Heat remaining 1 tablespoon oil in skillet over medium-high heat. Add onion, bell pepper, carrots and garlic; cook and stir until onion is just tender but not brown. Add to **CROCK-POT®** slow cooker. Stir in rice, chili powder and remaining ½ teaspoon salt.

4. Drain tomatoes over 1-quart measuring cup, reserving juice. Add vegetable broth to tomato juice. Add enough water to measure 4 cups. Pour into **CROCK-POT®** slow cooker. Stir in tomatoes; top with eggplant. Cover; cook on LOW 3½ to 4 hours or until rice is tender and liquid is absorbed.

Makes 8 servings

Nutrition Information

Serving Size: 1 cup

Calories 238
Total Fat 8g
Saturated Fat 1g
Protein 6g
Carbohydrate 37g
Cholesterol 1mg
Fiber 4g
Sodium..................693mg

Dietary Exchanges:
2 Starch, 1 Vegetable,
1½ Fat

Mixed Grain Tabbouleh

- 3 cups chicken broth
- 1 cup uncooked long grain brown rice
- ½ cup uncooked bulgur wheat
- 1 cup chopped tomatoes
- ½ cup minced green onions
- ¼ cup chopped fresh mint
- ¼ cup chopped fresh basil
- ¼ cup chopped fresh oregano
- 3 tablespoons lemon juice
- 3 tablespoons olive oil
- ½ teaspoon salt
- ½ teaspoon black pepper
  Sprigs fresh mint (optional)

1. Combine broth, rice and bulgur in **CROCK-POT**® slow cooker. Cover; cook on LOW 7 hours or on HIGH 2½ to 3 hours or until rice and bulgur are tender.

2. Combine tomatoes, green onions, mint, basil, oregano, lemon juice, oil, salt and pepper in large bowl. Stir cooked rice and bulgur into tomato mixture. Cool completely before serving.

Makes 6 servings

Spinach Risotto

2 teaspoons unsalted butter

2 teaspoons olive oil

3 tablespoons finely chopped shallot

1¼ cups uncooked Arborio rice

½ cup dry white wine

3 cups fat-free reduced-sodium chicken broth

½ teaspoon salt

2 cups baby spinach

¼ cup grated Parmesan cheese

2 tablespoons pine nuts, toasted*

To toast pine nuts, spread in single layer in heavy skillet. Cook over medium heat 1 to 2 minutes or until nuts are lightly browned, stirring frequently.

1. Melt butter in medium skillet over medium heat; add oil. Add shallot; cook and stir until softened but not browned.

2. Stir in rice; cook 2 to 3 minutes or until well coated. Stir in wine; cook until reduced by half.

3. Remove rice mixture to **CROCK-POT**® slow cooker. Stir in broth and salt. Cover; cook on HIGH 2 to 2½ hours or until rice is almost cooked but still contains a little liquid.

4. Stir in spinach. Cover; cook on HIGH 15 to 20 minutes or until spinach is cooked and rice is tender and creamy. Gently stir in cheese and pine nuts just before serving.

Makes 4 servings

Serving Size:
about ¾ cup

Calories 118
Total Fat 3g
Saturated Fat 1g
Protein 6g
Carbohydrate 20g
Cholesterol 0mg
Fiber 6g
Sodium.................521mg

Dietary Exchanges:
1 Starch, 1 Vegetable,
½ Fat

Hot Three-Bean Casserole

2 **tablespoons olive oil**

1 **cup coarsely chopped onion**

1 **cup chopped celery**

2 **cloves garlic, minced**

1 **can (about 15 ounces) chickpeas, rinsed and drained**

1 **can (about 15 ounces) kidney beans, rinsed and drained**

1 **package (10 ounces) frozen cut green beans**

1 **cup water**

1 **cup coarsely chopped tomato**

1 **can (8 ounces) tomato sauce**

1 **to 2 jalapeño peppers, seeded and minced***

1 **tablespoon chili powder**

2 **teaspoons sugar**

1½ **teaspoons ground cumin**

1 **teaspoon salt**

1 **teaspoon dried oregano**

¼ **teaspoon black pepper**

Sprigs fresh oregano (optional)

*Jalapeño peppers can sting and irritate the skin, so wear rubber gloves when handling peppers and do not touch your eyes.

1. Heat oil in large skillet over medium heat. Add onion, celery and garlic; cook and stir 5 minutes or until tender. Place in **CROCK-POT**® slow cooker.

2. Add chickpeas, beans, water, tomato, tomato sauce, jalapeño pepper, chili powder, sugar, cumin, salt, dried oregano and black pepper to **CROCK-POT**® slow cooker; stir to blend. Cover; cook on LOW 6 to 8 hours. Garnish with fresh oregano.

Makes 12 servings

Nutrition Information

Serving Size: ¾ cup

Calories 250
Total Fat 8g
Saturated Fat 3g
Protein 5g
Carbohydrate 43g
Cholesterol 60mg
Fiber 3g
Sodium................. 240mg

Dietary Exchanges:
2 Starch, 1½ Fat

Sweet Potato and Pecan Casserole

- **1 can (40 ounces) sweet potatoes, drained and mashed**
- **½ cup apple juice**
- **4 tablespoons unsalted butter, melted and divided**
- **½ teaspoon salt**
- **½ teaspoon ground cinnamon**
- **¼ teaspoon black pepper**
- **2 eggs, beaten**
- **⅓ cup packed brown sugar**
- **¼ cup chopped pecans**
- **2 tablespoons all-purpose flour**

1. Combine potatoes, apple juice, 2 tablespoons butter, salt, cinnamon and pepper in large bowl. Beat in eggs. Place mixture into **CROCK-POT®** slow cooker.

2. Combine brown sugar, pecans, flour and remaining 2 tablespoons butter in small bowl. Spread over potatoes in **CROCK-POT®** slow cooker. Cover; cook on HIGH 3 to 4 hours.

Makes 8 servings

Candied Sweet Potatoes

3 medium sweet potatoes (1½ to 2 pounds), sliced into
   ½-inch rounds

½ cup water

¼ cup (½ stick) butter, cut into pieces

10 packets sugar substitute

1 tablespoon vanilla

1 teaspoon ground nutmeg

Combine potatoes, water, butter, sugar substitute, vanilla and nutmeg
in **CROCK-POT**® slow cooker; mix well. Cover; cook on LOW
7 hours or on HIGH 4 hours or until potatoes are tender.

Makes 4 servings

Mashed Rutabagas and Potatoes

- 2 **pounds rutabagas, peeled and cut into ½-inch pieces**
- 1 **pound potatoes, peeled and cut into ½-inch pieces**
- ½ **cup low-fat (1%) milk**
- ½ **teaspoon ground nutmeg**
- 2 **tablespoons chopped fresh Italian parsley**
  Sprigs fresh Italian parsley (optional)

1. Place rutabagas and potatoes in **CROCK-POT**® slow cooker; add enough water to cover vegetables. Cover; cook on LOW 6 hours or on HIGH 3 hours. Remove vegetables to large bowl using slotted spoon. Discard cooking liquid.

2. Mash vegetables with potato masher. Add milk, nutmeg and chopped parsley; stir until smooth. Garnish with parsley sprigs.

Makes 8 servings

Nutrition Information

Serving Size: 1⅓ cups

Calories 93
Total Fat 1g
Saturated Fat 1g
Protein 3g
Carbohydrate 20g
Cholesterol 1mg
Fiber 3g
Sodium....................30mg

Dietary Exchanges:
½ Starch, 2 Vegetable

Serving Size: ½ squash with about ¼ cup rice mixture

Calories 130
Total Fat.........................1g
Saturated Fat 0g
Protein 2g
Carbohydrate 30g
Cholesterol 0mg
Fiber 4g
Sodium.................... 10mg

Dietary Exchanges:
1½ Starch, 3½ Vegetable

Cran-Orange Acorn Squash

 5 **tablespoons uncooked instant brown rice**
 3 **tablespoons minced onion**
 3 **tablespoons diced celery**
 3 **tablespoons dried cranberries**
    Pinch ground sage
 3 **small acorn or carnival squash, halved and seeded**
 1 **teaspoon unsalted butter, cubed**
 9 **teaspoons orange juice**
 ½ **cup warm water**

1. Combine rice, onion, celery, cranberries and sage in small bowl. Stuff each of the squash halves evenly with rice mixture; dot with butter. Pour 1½ teaspoons orange juice over stuffing on each of the squash halves.

2. Stand squash in **CROCK-POT®** slow cooker. Pour water into bottom of **CROCK-POT®** slow cooker. Cover; cook on LOW 2½ hours or until squash is tender.

Makes 6 servings

Mediterranean Red Potatoes

3 medium unpeeled red potatoes, cubed
⅔ cup fresh or frozen pearl onions
  Garlic-flavored cooking spray
¾ teaspoon Italian seasoning
¼ teaspoon black pepper
1 small tomato, seeded and chopped
2 ounces feta cheese, crumbled
2 tablespoons chopped black olives

1. Place potatoes and onions in 1½-quart soufflé dish that fits inside of **CROCK-POT**® slow cooker. Spray with garlic-flavored cooking spray; toss to coat. Add Italian seasoning and pepper; mix well. Cover dish tightly with foil.

2. Make foil handles using three 18×3-inch strips of heavy-duty foil or use regular foil folded to double thickness. Crisscross foil in spoke design; place across bottom and up side of stoneware. Place soufflé dish in center of strips in **CROCK-POT**® slow cooker. Pull foil strips up and over dish.

3. Pour hot water into **CROCK-POT**® slow cooker to about 1½ inches from top of soufflé dish. Cover; cook on LOW 7 to 8 hours.

4. Use foil handles to lift dish out of **CROCK-POT**® slow cooker. Stir tomato, cheese and olives into potato mixture.

Makes 4 servings

Chunky Ranch Potatoes

Nutrition Information

Serving Size: about 1 cup

Calories 200
Total Fat.......................8g
Saturated Fat 1g
Protein 3g
Carbohydrate 28g
Cholesterol 5mg
Fiber 3g
Sodium.................150mg

Dietary Exchanges:
1½ Fat

- **3 pounds unpeeled red potatoes, quartered**
- **1 cup water**
- **½ cup prepared ranch dressing**
- **½ cup grated Parmesan or Cheddar cheese (optional)**
- **¼ cup minced fresh chives**

1. Place potatoes in **CROCK-POT®** slow cooker. Add water. Cover; cook on LOW 7 to 9 hours or on HIGH 4 to 6 hours.

2. Stir in ranch dressing, cheese and chives. Break up potatoes into large pieces.

Makes 8 servings

Mushroom Wild Rice

- **1½ cups fat-free reduced-sodium chicken broth**
- **1 cup uncooked wild rice**
- **½ cup diced onion**
- **½ cup sliced mushrooms**
- **½ cup diced red or green bell pepper**
- **1 tablespoon olive oil**
- **¼ teaspoon salt**
- **¼ teaspoon black pepper**

Place broth, rice, onion, mushrooms, bell pepper, oil, salt and black pepper in **CROCK-POT®** slow cooker. Cover; cook on HIGH 2½ hours or until rice is tender and liquid is absorbed.

Makes 8 servings

Nutrition Information

Serving Size: ½ cup

Calories 100
Total Fat 2g
Saturated Fat 1g
Protein 4g
Carbohydrate 17g
Cholesterol 5mg
Fiber 2g
Sodium 148mg

Dietary Exchanges:
1 Starch, ½ Fat

Asian Kale and Chickpeas

Nutrition Information

Serving Size:
about 1¾ cups

Calories 280
Total Fat 5g
Saturated Fat 1g
Protein 14g
Carbohydrate 47g
Cholesterol 0mg
Fiber 11g
Sodium................. 330mg

Dietary Exchanges:
2½ Starch, 1 Vegetable,
1 Meat, ½ Fat

- **1 tablespoon sesame oil**
- **1 medium onion, thinly sliced**
- **2 teaspoons grated fresh ginger**
- **2 cloves garlic, minced**
- **2 jalapeño peppers, chopped***
- **8 cups chopped kale**
- **1 cup reduced-sodium vegetable broth**
- **2 cans (about 15 ounces *each*) unsalted chickpeas, rinsed and drained**
- **1 tablespoon lime juice**
- **1 teaspoon grated lime peel**
- **2 cups hot cooked rice (optional)**

Jalapeño peppers can sting and irritate the skin, so wear rubber gloves when handling peppers and do not touch your eyes.

1. Coat inside of **CROCK-POT**® slow cooker with nonstick cooking spray. Heat oil in large skillet over medium-high heat. Add onion, ginger, garlic and jalapeño peppers; cook 1 minute. Add kale; cook and stir 2 minutes or until slightly wilted. Remove kale mixture to **CROCK-POT**® slow cooker. Add broth and chickpeas.

2. Cover; cook on LOW 3 hours. Turn off heat. Stir in lime juice and lime peel. Serve with rice, if desired.

Makes 4 servings

Tip

It's easy to prepare these potatoes ahead of time. Simply follow the recipe and then turn off the heat. Let it stand at room temperature for up to 2 hours. You may reheat or serve the potatoes at room temperature.

Lemon-Mint Red Potatoes

2 **pounds new red potatoes**

3 **tablespoons extra virgin olive oil**

1 **teaspoon salt**

¾ **teaspoon Greek seasoning or dried oregano**

¼ **teaspoon garlic powder**

¼ **teaspoon black pepper**

¼ **cup chopped fresh mint, divided**

2 **tablespoons lemon juice**

1 **teaspoon grated lemon peel**

1 **tablespoon unsalted butter**

1. Coat inside of **CROCK-POT®** slow cooker with nonstick cooking spray. Combine potatoes and oil in **CROCK-POT®** slow cooker; toss gently to coat. Sprinkle with salt, Greek seasoning, garlic powder and pepper. Cover; cook on LOW 7 hours or on HIGH 4 hours.

2. Add 2 tablespoons mint, lemon juice, lemon peel, and butter; stir until butter is completely melted. Cover; cook on HIGH 15 minutes. Garnish with remaining 2 tablespoons mint.

Makes 6 servings

Nutrition Information

Serving Size: ½ cup

Calories 70
Total Fat 3g
Saturated Fat 1g
Protein 3g
Carbohydrate 7g
Cholesterol 5mg
Fiber 2g
Sodium................ 340mg

Dietary Exchanges:
½ Fat, 1 Vegetable

Barley and Vegetable Risotto

2 teaspoons olive oil
1 small onion, diced
8 ounces sliced mushrooms
¾ cup uncooked pearl barley
1 large red bell pepper, diced
4½ cups fat-free reduced-sodium vegetable broth
2 cups packed baby spinach
¼ cup grated Parmesan cheese
¼ teaspoon black pepper

1. Heat oil in large skillet over medium-high heat. Add onion; cook and stir 2 minutes or until lightly browned. Add mushrooms; cook and stir 5 minutes or until mushrooms have released their liquid and are just beginning to brown. Remove to **CROCK-POT**® slow cooker.

2. Add barley and bell pepper to **CROCK-POT**® slow cooker; pour in broth. Cover; cook on LOW 4 to 5 hours or on HIGH 2½ to 3 hours or until barley is tender and liquid is absorbed.

3. Stir in spinach. Turn off heat. Let stand 5 minutes. Gently stir in cheese and black pepper just before serving.

Makes 6 servings

Nutrition Information

Serving Size: about
¾ cup

Calories 190
Total Fat.........................5g
Saturated Fat...............3g
Protein 5g
Carbohydrate 31g
Cholesterol 15mg
Fiber 4g
Sodium..................610mg

Dietary Exchanges:
1 Fat

Rustic Garlic Mashed Potatoes

2 pounds baking potatoes, unpeeled and cut into ½-inch cubes

¼ cup water

2 tablespoons unsalted butter, cubed

1¼ teaspoons salt

½ teaspoon garlic powder

¼ teaspoon black pepper

1 cup fat-free (skim) milk

Place potatoes, water, butter, salt, garlic powder and pepper in **CROCK-POT**® slow cooker; toss to combine. Cover; cook on LOW 7 hours or on HIGH 4 hours. Add milk to potatoes. Mash potatoes with potato masher until smooth.

Makes 5 servings

Coconut-Lime Sweet Potatoes with Walnuts

2½ **pounds sweet potatoes, cut into 1-inch pieces**

  8 **ounces shredded carrots**

¾ **cup shredded coconut, toasted and divided***

  1 **tablespoon unsalted butter, melted**

  3 **tablespoons sugar**

½ **teaspoon salt**

  3 **tablespoons walnuts, toasted and coarsely chopped****

  2 **teaspoons grated lime peel**

To toast coconut, spread evenly on ungreased baking sheet. Toast in preheated 350°F oven 5 to 7 minutes or until light golden brown, stirring occasionally.

**To toast walnuts, spread in single layer in small skillet. Cook and stir over medium heat 1 to 2 minutes or until nuts are lightly browned.*

1. Combine potatoes, carrots, ½ cup coconut, butter, sugar and salt in **CROCK-POT®** slow cooker. Cover; cook on LOW 5 to 6 hours. Remove to large bowl.

2. Mash potatoes with potato masher. Stir in walnuts and lime peel. Sprinkle with remaining ¼ cup coconut.

Makes 8 servings

VEGETABLE SIDES

Sunshine Squash

1 **butternut squash (about 2 pounds), peeled, seeded and diced**

1 **can (about 15 ounces) corn, drained**

1 **can (about 14 ounces) diced tomatoes**

1 **medium onion, coarsely chopped**

1 **medium green bell pepper, cut into 1-inch pieces**

½ **cup fat-free reduced-sodium chicken broth**

1 **canned mild green chile, coarsely chopped**

1 **clove garlic, minced**

½ **teaspoon salt**

¼ **teaspoon black pepper**

1 **tablespoon plus 1½ teaspoons tomato paste**

1. Combine squash, corn, tomatoes, onion, bell pepper, broth, chile, garlic, salt and black pepper in **CROCK-POT®** slow cooker; stir to blend. Cover; cook on LOW 6 hours or until squash is tender.

2. Turn **CROCK-POT®** slow cooker to HIGH. Remove about ¼ cup cooking liquid and blend with tomato paste in small bowl. Stir into **CROCK-POT®** slow cooker. Cover; cook on HIGH 30 minutes or until mixture is slightly thickened and heated through.

Makes 6 to 8 servings

Nutrition Information

Serving Size: 1 cup

Calories 170
Total Fat 1g
Saturated Fat 0g
Protein 5g
Carbohydrate 39g
Cholesterol 0mg
Fiber 5g
Sodium 640mg

Dietary Exchanges:
3½ Starch, 4 Vegetable

Nutrition Information

Serving Size: 1 cup

Calories 150
Total Fat.......................5g
Saturated Fat...............3g
Protein 5g
Carbohydrate 23g
Cholesterol 10mg
Fiber 3g
Sodium................. 270mg

Dietary Exchanges:
1 Starch, 1 Fat

Escalloped Corn

2 **tablespoons unsalted butter**
½ **cup chopped onion**
3 **tablespoons all-purpose flour**
1 **cup fat-free (skim) milk**
4 **cups frozen corn, thawed and divided**
½ **teaspoon salt**
½ **teaspoon dried thyme**
¼ **teaspoon black pepper**
⅛ **teaspoon ground nutmeg**
Sprigs fresh thyme (optional)

1. Melt butter in small saucepan over medium heat. Add onion; cook and stir 5 minutes or until tender. Add flour; cook and stir 1 minute. Stir in milk. Bring to a boil; cook and stir 1 minute or until thickened.

2. Process 2 cups corn in food processor or blender until coarsely chopped. Combine milk mixture, chopped corn and remaining 2 cups whole corn, salt, dried thyme, pepper and nutmeg in **CROCK-POT®** slow cooker; mix well. Cover; cook on LOW 3½ to 4 hours. Garnish with fresh thyme.

Makes 6 servings

Tarragon Carrots in White Wine

Nutrition Information

Serving Size: ½ cup

Calories 80
Total Fat.......................0g
Saturated Fat 0g
Protein 2g
Carbohydrate 16g
Cholesterol 0mg
Fiber 3g
Sodium................. 150mg

Dietary Exchanges:
1 Starch, 2 Vegetable

½ **cup fat-free chicken broth**
½ **cup dry white wine**
1 **tablespoon lemon juice**
1 **tablespoon minced fresh tarragon**
2 **teaspoons finely chopped green onions**
1½ **teaspoons chopped fresh Italian parsley**
1 **clove garlic, minced**
1 **teaspoon salt**
8 **medium carrots, cut into matchsticks**
2 **tablespoons melba toast, crushed**
2 **tablespoons cold water**

1. Combine broth, wine, lemon juice, tarragon, green onions, parsley, garlic and salt in **CROCK-POT®** slow cooker. Add carrots; stir well to combine. Cover; cook on LOW 2½ to 3 hours or on HIGH 1½ to 2 hours.

2. Dissolve toast crumbs in water in small bowl; add to carrots. Cover; cook on LOW 10 minutes or until thickened.

Makes 6 servings

Nutrition Information

Serving Size: ¾ cup

Calories 150
Total Fat......................12g
Saturated Fat...............3g
Protein 4g
Carbohydrate 8g
Cholesterol 5mg
Fiber 2g
Sodium................. 370mg

Dietary Exchanges:
1½ Vegetable, 2 Fat

Roasted Summer Squash with Pine Nuts and Romano Cheese

- **2 tablespoons extra virgin olive oil**
- **½ cup chopped yellow onion**
- **1 medium red bell pepper, chopped**
- **1 clove garlic, minced**
- **3 medium zucchini, cut into ½-inch slices**
- **3 medium summer squash, cut into ½-inch slices**
- **½ cup chopped pine nuts**
- **⅓ cup grated Romano cheese**
- **1 teaspoon Italian seasoning**
- **1 teaspoon salt**
- **¼ teaspoon black pepper**
- **1 tablespoon unsalted butter, cubed**

1. Heat oil in large skillet over medium-high heat. Add onion, bell pepper and garlic; cook and stir 10 minutes or until onion is translucent and soft. Remove to **CROCK-POT®** slow cooker.

2. Add zucchini and summer squash. Toss lightly.

3. Combine pine nuts, cheese, Italian seasoning, salt and black pepper in small bowl. Fold half of cheese mixture into squash. Sprinkle remaining cheese mixture on top. Dot cheese with butter. Cover; cook on LOW 4 to 6 hours.

Makes 8 servings

Spinach Artichoke Gratin

Nutrition Information

Serving Size: ⅔ cup

Calories	125
Total Fat	1g
Saturated Fat	1g
Protein	15g
Carbohydrate	13g
Cholesterol	6mg
Fiber	5g
Sodium	537mg

Dietary Exchanges:
1 Vegetable, 2 Meat

2 cups (16 ounces) fat-free cottage cheese

½ cup cholesterol-free egg substitute

4½ tablespoons grated Parmesan cheese, divided

1 tablespoon lemon juice

⅛ teaspoon ground nutmeg

⅛ teaspoon black pepper

2 packages (10 ounces *each*) frozen chopped spinach, thawed and squeezed dry

⅓ cup thinly sliced green onions

1 package (10 ounces) frozen artichoke hearts, thawed and halved

1. Add cottage cheese, egg substitute, 3 tablespoons Parmesan cheese, lemon juice, nutmeg and pepper to food processor or blender; process until smooth.

2. Coat inside of **CROCK-POT**® slow cooker with nonstick cooking spray. Combine spinach, cottage cheese mixture and green onions in large bowl. Spread half of mixture in **CROCK-POT**® slow cooker.

3. Pat artichoke halves dry with paper towels. Place in single layer over spinach mixture. Sprinkle with remaining 1½ tablespoons Parmesan cheese. Cover with remaining spinach mixture. Cover; cook on LOW 3 to 3½ hours or on HIGH 2 to 2½ hours.

Makes 6 servings

Caponata

1 **medium eggplant (about 1 pound), peeled and cut into ½-inch pieces**

1 **can (about 14 ounces) diced tomatoes**

1 **medium onion, chopped**

1 **red bell pepper, cut into ½-inch pieces**

½ **cup medium salsa**

¼ **cup extra virgin olive oil**

2 **tablespoons capers, drained**

2 **tablespoons balsamic vinegar**

3 **cloves garlic, minced**

1 **teaspoon dried oregano**

⅓ **cup packed fresh basil, cut into thin strips**

2 **loaves (24 slices) Italian or French bread, sliced and toasted**

1. Mix eggplant, tomatoes, onion, bell pepper, salsa, oil, capers, vinegar, garlic and oregano in **CROCK-POT®** slow cooker. Cover; cook on LOW 7 to 8 hours or until vegetables are crisp-tender.

2. Stir in basil. Serve at room temperature with toasted bread.

Makes about 5¼ cups

Beets in Spicy Mustard Sauce

Serving Size: 1½ cups

Calories 116
Total Fat 2g
Saturated Fat 0g
Protein 4g
Carbohydrate 21g
Cholesterol 6mg
Fiber 6g
Sodium................... 253mg

Dietary Exchanges:
3½ Vegetable, ½ Fat

3 **pounds beets, peeled, halved and cut into ½-inch slices**
¼ **cup reduced-fat sour cream**
2 **tablespoons spicy brown mustard**
2 **teaspoons lemon juice**
2 **cloves garlic, minced**
¼ **teaspoon black pepper**
⅛ **teaspoon dried thyme**

1. Place beets in **CROCK-POT**® slow cooker. Add enough water to cover by 1 inch. Cover; cook on LOW 7 to 8 hours or until beets are tender.

2. Combine sour cream, mustard, lemon juice, garlic, pepper and thyme in small bowl. Spoon over beets; toss to coat. Cover; cook on LOW 15 minutes.

Makes 4 servings

Nutrition Information

Serving Size: ½ cup

Calories 76
Total Fat 3g
Saturated Fat 1g
Protein 2g
Carbohydrate 12g
Cholesterol 0mg
Fiber 4g
Sodium 194mg

Dietary Exchanges:
2 Vegetable, ½ Fat

Fennel Braised with Tomato

2 **bulbs fennel**

1 **tablespoon olive oil**

1 **onion, sliced**

1 **clove garlic, sliced**

4 **tomatoes, chopped**

⅔ **cup reduced-sodium vegetable broth**

3 **tablespoons dry white wine**

1 **tablespoon chopped fresh marjoram** *or* **1 teaspoon dried marjoram**

¼ **teaspoon salt**

¼ **teaspoon black pepper**

1. Trim stems and bottoms from fennel bulbs, reserving green leafy tops for garnish. Cut each bulb lengthwise into four wedges.

2. Heat oil in large skillet over medium heat. Add fennel, onion and garlic; cook and stir 5 minutes or until onion is soft and translucent.

3. Combine tomatoes, broth, wine, marjoram, salt and black pepper in **CROCK-POT®** slow cooker; stir to blend. Cover; cook on LOW 2 to 3 hours or on HIGH 1 to 1½ hours or until vegetables are tender. Garnish with reserved fennel leaves.

Makes 6 servings

Garlicky Mustard Greens

Nutrition Information

Serving Size: 1½ cups

Calories 72
Total Fat 2g
Saturated Fat 1g
Protein 6g
Carbohydrate 11g
Cholesterol 0mg
Fiber 5g
Sodium 42mg

Dietary Exchanges:
2½ Vegetable

- **2** **pounds mustard greens**
- **1** **teaspoon olive oil**
- **1** **cup chopped onion**
- **2** **cloves garlic, minced**
- **¾** **cup chopped red bell pepper**
- **½** **cup fat-free reduced-sodium vegetable broth**
- **1** **tablespoon cider vinegar**
- **1** **teaspoon sugar**

1. Remove stems and any wilted leaves from greens. Stack several leaves; roll up. Cut crosswise into 1-inch slices. Repeat with remaining greens.

2. Heat oil in large saucepan over medium heat. Add onion and garlic; cook and stir 5 minutes or until onion is tender. Combine mustard greens mixture, bell pepper and broth in **CROCK-POT**® slow cooker. Cover; cook on LOW 3 to 4 hours or on HIGH 2 hours.

3. Combine vinegar and sugar in small bowl; stir until sugar is dissolved. Stir into cooked greens; serve immediately.

Makes 4 servings

Brussels Sprouts with Bacon, Thyme and Raisins

Nutrition Information

Serving Size: ¾ cup

Calories 109
Total Fat........................2g
Saturated Fat 1g
Protein 6g
Carbohydrate 21g
Cholesterol 3mg
Fiber 5g
Sodium..................110mg

Dietary Exchanges:
1½ Starch

- **2 pounds Brussels sprouts**
- **1 cup reduced-sodium chicken broth**
- **⅔ cup golden raisins**
- **2 thick slices applewood smoked bacon, chopped**
- **2 tablespoons chopped fresh thyme**

Trim ends from sprouts; cut in half lengthwise through core (or in quarters). Combine sprouts, broth, raisins, bacon and thyme in **CROCK-POT**® slow cooker. Cover; cook on LOW 3 to 4 hours.

Makes 8 servings

Collard Greens

1 **tablespoon olive oil**

3 **turkey necks**

5 **bunches collard greens, stemmed and chopped**

5 **cups reduced-sodium chicken broth**

1 **small onion, chopped**

2 **cloves garlic, minced**

1 **tablespoon cider vinegar**

1 **teaspoon sugar**

1 **teaspoon red pepper flakes**

1. Heat oil in large skillet over medium-high heat. Add turkey necks; cook and stir 3 to 5 minutes or until brown.

2. Combine turkey necks, collard greens, broth, onion and garlic in **CROCK-POT** slow cooker. Cover; cook on LOW 5 to 6 hours. Remove and discard turkey necks. Stir in vinegar, sugar and red pepper flakes.

Makes 6 servings

Slow-Good Apples and Carrots

6 **carrots, sliced into ½-inch slices**

4 **apples, peeled, cored and sliced**

¼ **cup plus 1 tablespoon all-purpose flour**

1 **tablespoon packed brown sugar**

½ **teaspoon ground nutmeg**

1 **tablespoon butter, cubed**

½ **cup orange juice**

Layer carrots and apples in **CROCK-POT**® slow cooker. Combine flour, brown sugar and nutmeg in small bowl; sprinkle over carrots and apples. Dot with butter; pour in orange juice. Cover; cook on LOW 3½ to 4 hours or until carrots are crisp-tender.

Makes 6 servings

Nutrition Information

Serving Size: ½ cup

Calories 62
Total Fat 1g
Saturated Fat 1g
Protein 1g
Carbohydrate 16g
Cholesterol 0mg
Fiber 2g
Sodium 191mg

Dietary Exchanges:
1 Vegetable, ½ Fruit

Sweet-Sour Cabbage with Apples and Caraway Seeds

4 cups shredded red cabbage

1 large tart apple, peeled, cored and cut crosswise into ¼-inch-thick slices

¼ cup packed light brown sugar

¼ cup water

¼ cup cider vinegar

½ teaspoon salt

¼ teaspoon caraway seeds

Dash black pepper

Combine cabbage, apple, brown sugar, water, vinegar, salt, caraway seeds and pepper in **CROCK-POT®** slow cooker; stir to blend. Cover; cook on LOW 2½ to 3 hours.

Makes 6 servings

Nutrition Information

Serving Size: about
1 cup

Calories 70
Total Fat......................4g
Saturated Fat 3g
Protein 3g
Carbohydrate 7g
Cholesterol 10mg
Fiber 3g
Sodium................400mg

Dietary Exchanges:
1 Vegetable, 1 Fat

Cauliflower Mash

2 heads cauliflower (8 cups florets)
1 tablespoon butter
1 tablespoon half-and-half
1 teaspoon salt
Sprigs fresh Italian parsley (optional)

1. Arrange cauliflower in **CROCK-POT**® slow cooker; add enough water to fill **CROCK-POT**® slow cooker about 2 inches. Cover; cook on LOW 5 to 6 hours. Drain well.

2. Place cooked cauliflower in food processor or blender; process until almost smooth. Add butter; process until smooth. Add half-and-half as needed to reach desired consistency. Season with salt. Garnish with parsley.

Makes 6 servings

Simmered Napa Cabbage with Dried Apricots

4 cups napa cabbage or green cabbage, cored, cleaned and sliced thin

1 cup chopped dried apricots

¼ cup clover honey

2 tablespoons orange juice

½ cup dry red wine

Salt and black pepper (optional)

Grated orange peel (optional)

1. Combine cabbage and apricots in **CROCK-POT®** slow cooker; toss to coat.

2. Combine honey and orange juice in small bowl; mix until smooth. Drizzle over cabbage. Add wine. Cover; cook on LOW 5 to 6 hours or on HIGH 2 to 3 hours.

3. Season with salt and pepper, if desired. Garnish with orange peel.

Makes 8 servings

French Carrot Medley

Serving Size: ⅔ cup

Calories 42
Total Fat.........................1g
Saturated Fat................1g
Protein 1g
Carbohydrate 10g
Cholesterol 0mg
Fiber 2g
Sodium...................118mg

Dietary Exchanges:
1 Vegetable, ½ Fruit

2	**cups sliced carrots**
¾	**cup unsweetened orange juice**
1	**can (4 ounces) sliced mushrooms, undrained**
4	**stalks celery, sliced**
2	**tablespoons chopped onion**
½	**teaspoon dried dill weed**
	Salt and black pepper
¼	**cup cold water**
2	**teaspoons cornstarch**

1. Combine carrots, orange juice, mushrooms, celery, onion, dill weed, salt and pepper in **CROCK-POT**® slow cooker. Cover; cook on LOW 3 to 4 hours or on HIGH 2 hours.

2. Stir water into cornstarch in small bowl until smooth. Whisk into cooking liquid in **CROCK-POT**® slow cooker. Cover; cook on HIGH 15 minutes or until sauce is thickened. Spoon sauce evenly over vegetable mixture before serving.

Makes 6 servings

Creamy Curried Spinach

Serving Size:
about ¼ cup

Calories 80
Total Fat 5g
Saturated Fat 3g
Protein 4g
Carbohydrate 7g
Cholesterol 10mg
Fiber 4g
Sodium 110mg

Dietary Exchanges:
1 Vegetable, ½ Fruit

- **3 packages (10 ounces *each*) frozen spinach, thawed**
- **1 onion, chopped**
- **4 teaspoons minced garlic**
- **2 tablespoons curry powder**
- **1 tablespoon unsalted butter, melted**
- **¼ cup fat-free chicken broth**
- **¼ cup light whipping cream**
- **1 teaspoon lemon juice**

Combine spinach, onion, garlic, curry powder, butter and broth in **CROCK-POT®** slow cooker. Cover; cook on LOW 3 to 4 hours or on HIGH 2 hours or until done. Stir in cream and lemon juice 30 minutes before end of cooking time.

Makes 8 servings

Polenta-Style Corn Casserole

Nutrition Information

Serving Size: 1 cup

Calories 150
Total Fat.......................5g
Saturated Fat...............3g
Protein 7g
Carbohydrate 19g
Cholesterol 15mg
Fiber 1g
Sodium.................800mg

Dietary Exchanges:
1 Starch, ½ Meat

1 can (about 14 ounces) fat-free chicken broth
½ cup cornmeal
1 can (7 ounces) corn, drained
1 can (4 ounces) diced mild green chiles, drained
¼ cup diced red bell pepper
½ teaspoon salt
¼ teaspoon black pepper
1 cup (4 ounces) shredded reduced-fat Cheddar cheese

1. Pour broth into **CROCK-POT**® slow cooker. Whisk in cornmeal. Add corn, chiles, bell pepper, salt and black pepper. Cover; cook on LOW 4 to 5 hours or on HIGH 2 to 3 hours.

2. Stir in cheese. Cook, uncovered, on HIGH 15 to 30 minutes or until cheese is melted.

Makes 6 servings

Supper Squash Medley

Nutrition Information

Serving Size: 1¼ cups

Calories	150
Total Fat	1g
Saturated Fat	0g
Protein	5g
Carbohydrate	32g
Cholesterol	0mg
Fiber	5g
Sodium	650mg

Dietary Exchanges:
2 Starch, 3½ Vegetable

2 butternut squash, peeled, seeded and diced (about 4 cups)
1 can (28 ounces) tomatoes, undrained
1 can (15 ounces) corn, drained
2 medium onions, chopped
2 medium green bell peppers, chopped
2 teaspoons minced garlic
2 green chiles, chopped
1 cup fat-free chicken broth
1 teaspoon salt
½ teaspoon black pepper
1 can (6 ounces) tomato paste

1. Combine squash, tomatoes, corn, onions, bell peppers, garlic, chiles, broth, salt and black pepper in **CROCK-POT**® slow cooker. Cover; cook on LOW 6 hours.

2. Remove about ½ cup cooking liquid and blend with tomato paste in small bowl. Whisk back into **CROCK-POT**® slow cooker. Cover; cook on HIGH 30 minutes or until mixture is slightly thickened and heated through.

Makes 8 servings

Nutrition Information

Serving Size: ¾ cup

Calories 140
Total Fat.......................0g
Saturated Fat 0g
Protein 1g
Carbohydrate 34g
Cholesterol 0mg
Fiber 2g
Sodium....................15mg

Dietary Exchanges:
2 Starch, ½ Vegetable

Red Cabbage and Apples

1 small head red cabbage, cored and thinly sliced
1 large apple, peeled and grated
¾ cup sugar
½ cup red wine vinegar
1 teaspoon ground cloves
Fresh apple slices (optional)

Combine cabbage, grated apple, sugar, vinegar and cloves in **CROCK-POT®** slow cooker; stir to blend. Cover; cook on HIGH 6 hours, stirring halfway through cooking time. Garnish with apple slices.

Makes 6 servings

INDEX

INDEX

METRIC CONVERSION CHART

VOLUME MEASUREMENTS (dry)

1/8 teaspoon = 0.5 mL
1/4 teaspoon = 1 mL
1/2 teaspoon = 2 mL
3/4 teaspoon = 4 mL
1 teaspoon = 5 mL
1 tablespoon = 15 mL
2 tablespoons = 30 mL
1/4 cup = 60 mL
1/3 cup = 75 mL
1/2 cup = 125 mL
2/3 cup = 150 mL
3/4 cup = 175 mL
1 cup = 250 mL
2 cups = 1 pint = 500 mL
3 cups = 750 mL
4 cups = 1 quart = 1 L

VOLUME MEASUREMENTS (fluid)

1 fluid ounce (2 tablespoons) = 30 mL
4 fluid ounces (1/2 cup) = 125 mL
8 fluid ounces (1 cup) = 250 mL
12 fluid ounces (1 1/2 cups) = 375 mL
16 fluid ounces (2 cups) = 500 mL

WEIGHTS (mass)

1/2 ounce = 15 g
1 ounce = 30 g
3 ounces = 90 g
4 ounces = 120 g
8 ounces = 225 g
10 ounces = 285 g
12 ounces = 360 g
16 ounces = 1 pound = 450 g

DIMENSIONS

1/16 inch = 2 mm
1/8 inch = 3 mm
1/4 inch = 6 mm
1/2 inch = 1.5 cm
3/4 inch = 2 cm
1 inch = 2.5 cm

OVEN TEMPERATURES

250°F = 120°C
275°F = 140°C
300°F = 150°C
325°F = 160°C
350°F = 180°C
375°F = 190°C
400°F = 200°C
425°F = 220°C
450°F = 230°C

BAKING PAN SIZES

Utensil	Size in Inches/Quarts	Metric Volume	Size in Centimeters
Baking or Cake Pan (square or rectangular)	8×8×2	2 L	20×20×5
	9×9×2	2.5 L	23×23×5
	12×8×2	3 L	30×20×5
	13×9×2	3.5 L	33×23×5
Loaf Pan	8×4×3	1.5 L	20×10×7
	9×5×3	2 L	23×13×7
Round Layer Cake Pan	8×1½	1.2 L	20×4
	9×1½	1.5 L	23×4
Pie Plate	8×1¼	750 mL	20×3
	9×1¼	1 L	23×3
Baking Dish or Casserole	1 quart	1 L	—
	1½ quart	1.5 L	—
	2 quart	2 L	—